Counselling
for Fertility
Problems

Counselling in Practice

Series editor: Windy Dryden
Associate editor: E. Thomas Dowd

Counselling in Practice is a series of books developed especially for counsellors and students of counselling which provides practical, accessible guidelines for dealing with clients with specific, but very common, problems.

Counselling for Fertility Problems

Jane Read

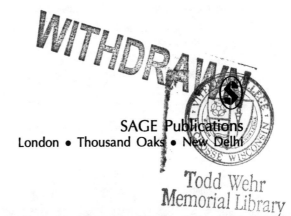

SAGE Publications
London • Thousand Oaks • New Delhi

First published 1995

 SAGE Publications Ltd
6 Bonhill Street
London EC2A 4PU

SAGE Publications Inc
2455 Teller Road
Thousand Oaks, California 91320

SAGE Publications India Pvt Ltd
32, M-Block Market
Greater Kailash – I
New Delhi 110 048

British Library Cataloguing in Publication data

A catalogue record for this book is available from the British Library.

ISBN 0 8039 8949 0
ISBN 0 8039 8950 4 (pbk)

Library of Congress catalog card number 95-067541

Typeset by Mayhew Typesetting, Rhayader, Powys
Printed in Great Britain by Biddles Ltd, Guildford, Surrey

For John Chaloner Ogle
1915–1992

Contents

Foreword

All I want is. . .
I feel such a failure. . .
Why me? Why us?

Twenty years ago, as a junior doctor, I resonated with my own sense of inadequacy when faced with such words. I wanted to make things better, I wanted success, I had been taught practical solutions. I had *not* learnt how to help others manage their feelings and was avoiding my own. The desk and my white coat protected me and the words 'team' and 'counsellor' were not in the textbook.

Fortunately, the management of fertility problems has moved on a long way since then. The science and technology may be challenging and fascinating, but no longer can we medicalise the situation and forget the whole person.

The impact of a fertility problem for the individual and the couple can be devastating. The task is to recognise the problem in the context of two adult sexual people with all their present emotions, past experiences and dreams of the future. In order to realise these dreams they have to have access to medical help, but they also have to manage their feelings and continue to function in the other aspects of their lives. This process continues from the moment of diagnosis through to the final outcome, whatever that might be. Today's successful management of fertility problems requires teamwork, with mutual understanding and respect for the variety of roles involved.

Books and articles on the medical aspects abound, so it is timely that here at last is a book to educate, support and guide all who are involved in counselling for fertility problems. I can remember how helpful I found Jane Read's insights when she shared with me her way of linking the stages of dealing with fertility problems to the stages of grieving described in the work of Dr Elizabeth Kubler-Ross on dying and William Worden on mourning. Suddenly, the reality of the process came home to me, the repeating mini-cycles of hope and grief that characterise the experience and delay the final letting go and moving on. Now Jane Read has expanded her ideas and put them into this book, together with her wealth of experience.

The book is clear and accessible, beginning with an overview of the counselling model for working with fertility problems. The model is carried through the chapters, supported by case examples that illustrate its application. Although primarily targeted at counsellors, I hope it will also be read by doctors and nurses as it offers the insights required of all members of a successful team.

Counselling for Fertility Problems is a book to encourage and support good practice.

Dr Fran Reader
Senior Lecturer in Human Sexuality
St George's Hospital Medical School

Acknowledgements

I gratefully acknowledge the Human Fertilisation and Embryology Authority for their permission to allow the full text of their leaflet *Sperm and Egg Donors and the Law* to be reproduced in the Appendices. Also, acknowledgement is due to HMSO for permission to reproduce excerpts from the Human Fertilisation and Embryology Acts (1990 and 1992) and the Abortion Act (1967) and Regulations (1991); and to Jossey-Bass Inc for permission to reproduce extracts from *Infertility and Pregnancy Loss. A Guide for Helping Professionals* by C.H. Shapiro.

Special thanks go to the couples and individuals whom I have worked with over the years, and who have taught me so much about the difficulties and processes that they undergo.

Thanks are also due to Windy Dryden, Series Editor at Sage Publications, for his help and support, as well as to Susan Worsey, for her encouragement, humour and generous gift of her time.

I offer a warm 'thank you' to the team at St George's Hospital (London) Human Sexuality Unit – that is, Margaret Ramage, Fran Reader, Eve Adler, Tor Lehmann, Bill Brind and Francis Guilfoyle – for support, encouragement and their willingness to allow me extra time to write this book. Particular thanks go to Anne Buggy for help with typing at the start of this project. My thanks go also to Peppy Macdonald at Fountain Books, Chiswick for help in literature searches, etc.

Lastly, I owe a big debt of gratitude to Ray Little, for his ideas, proof-reading, support and his love through all.

Glossary of terms

AID	artificial insemination by donor
AIH(P)	artificial insemination by husband (partner)
Azoospermia	absence of sperm in the semen
Cryo-preservation	the preservation by freezing of ova, sperm or embryos
Cytoplasm	the centre of the egg
DI	donor insemination
ET	embryo transfer
Gametes	sperm/ovum
GIFT	gamete intra-fallopian transfer
HFEA	Human Fertilisation and Embryology Authority
HFEA 1990	Human Fertilisation and Embryology Act 1990
ICM	Infertility Counselling Model
ICSI	intra-cytoplasmic sperm injection: a procedure to inject a single sperm into the cytoplasm of the egg
IVF	in vitro fertilisation
Oligospermia	a low sperm count, usually with higher than average levels of abnormal forms
Oocyte	an egg from an ovarian follicle
Peri-menopausal	the time period previous to the end of the menopause when a woman is likely to be ovulating irregularly
Post-menopausal	the time after the menopause has been completed, and the woman is no longer producing her own eggs
SUZI	sub-zonal insemination: a way of assisting fertilisation using direct insertion of usually less than 10 sperm under the zona pellucida

Introduction

This book is concerned with the counselling needs of those who have a fertility problem. By this I mean not only those who find that the pregnancy and child or children for whom they long do not come easily (or at all) to them, but also those who find that conception has occurred at a time, or in a particular circumstance or relationship when they are unprepared or unwilling to continue the pregnancy. The distress caused by either of these situations may be deep and intense.

> Neither pregnancy nor its absence is inherently desirable. The occurrence of a pregnancy can be met with joy or despair, and its absence can be a cause of relief or anguish. Whether or not these states are wanted, the conscious or unconscious meanings attached to pregnancy and infertility, the responses of others, the perceived implications of these states, and one's expectations for the future all are critical factors in determining an individual's response. (Adler, 1991: vii)

The way in which counselling may be helpful or otherwise, and the forms that that counselling might take, are the areas for discussion and examination in this book. The theory that underpins particular strategies and interventions is offered in Chapters 2–5 in particular. Here, I have used Egan's three-stage model of helping from *The Skilled Helper* (1981) as developed by Inskipp (1986), rather than Egan's recent 1993 version. This is because I prefer the clarity of the 1981 work.

For the sake of simplicity, I have limited the discussion of abortion to Chapter 6, which concentrates on the work involved in the counselling of individuals and couples who are seeking a termination of pregnancy, whether this be a wanted, planned, unplanned or unwanted pregnancy. However, as I indicated above and will go on to discuss in Chapter 1, there are, in terms of counselling, many common threads of issues and feelings that run through both infertility and abortion counselling. I am aware that this is a contentious view, and possibly offensive to some people. There is, however, useful learning to be had from the work that abortion counsellors have done since the Abortion Act of 1967 in

Britain and since the landmark case of *Roe* v. *Wade* in 1973, which set the constitutional and legal status of abortion in the United States.

There has been much discussion about the psychological 'causes' or aetiology of infertility, some of this to the effect that lack of fertility is indicative of some deep conflict over the maternal role. Little has been said about how this might also pertain to the paternal role, except in so far as retarded ejaculation is concerned. 'Common' examples of people who, after years of infertility, adopt a child only to conceive shortly thereafter are cited and have passed into the mythology surrounding infertility. For many this has added to the hurt and isolation that they experience as a result of their infertile state. There is little support for this in the literature, however:

> In general, reviewers of this literature on psychogenesis have concluded that the preponderance of studies reveals no consistent or striking evidence for psychological causes of infertility (Bents, 1985; Denber, 1978; Edelman and Connolly, 1986; Noyes and Chapnick, 1964). In addition, the related hypothesis that adoption facilitates conception by relieving emotional distress failed to receive support in several studies (Aaronson and Glienke, 1963; Edelmann and Connolly, 1986; Rock et al., 1965; Seibal and Taymor, 1982; Tyler et al., 1960). (Stanton and Dunkel-Schetter, 1991: 7)

The converse does occasionally appear to operate, that despite all precautions there must have been a subconscious or unconscious desire to get pregnant, and that this is the explanation for unplanned pregnancy. This also creates a sense of the woman (rather than the man), being at the mercy of her drives and desires. In turn this may leave the woman and her partner feeling out of control, helpless and somehow *at fault* in their situation. Guilt, shame and a sense of blame are frequently described by women and couples who have a problem related to their fertility, and this book will, I hope, help to ensure that clients or patients are understood by the professionals with whom they come into contact, and treated with the respect which all who need help with a difficulty or problem deserve.

The sexual difficulties and stresses that may result from infertility, or indeed may be the part cause of infertility, are discussed further in Chapter 7.

The special skills that are needed by the counsellor in working with couples, as well as the issues that are raised in this work, are explored in Chapter 8.

Issues that are raised by the use of donated gametes, including whether to tell the child, and clients' concerns about carrying a child whose genetic make up is half unknown, and the particular needs of donors, are explored in Chapters 9 and 10.

The literature on the response to a diagnosis of infertility has been linked with the literature on the response to trauma and bereavement and this book also makes that connection to a great extent.

Ethical issues

This book is, as stated, concerned with the needs of those who present with a fertility problem of some kind. It is not my intention to address in any depth the ethical and moral dilemmas that face not only those who work within abortion or infertility services, but also those who find themselves in the position of requiring such services. This is a large task, since the technological advances in infertility and abortion treatments, as well as new understandings and questions about the experience of the foetus in utero, challenge us almost daily. However, it is the duty and responsibility of helping professionals who confront these issues every day to develop an awareness of them, to be concerned with understanding for themselves particular areas of conflict or difficulty, and to be constantly willing to re-examine their own opinions and feelings. Above all, it is incumbent upon counsellors in particular, having clarified their views, to work with the client or patient in a way that is as free from personal prejudice and judgement as possible. It is also the responsibility of counsellors in such situations to be clear about their willingness or otherwise to work with certain client groups.

The case material in this book is based on my clinical practice, however, names and circumstances have been altered in order to ensure clients' anonymity.

1
The Development and Context of Fertility Counselling

This chapter will explore the development of counselling services for infertility and for abortion provision, and show how the two different contexts share a common framework for counselling the individual or couple who present with difficulties concerning their fertility. The legal and social contexts in which these services exist and operate will also be discussed. Brief discussions of the overlapping areas of adoption, genetic counselling, the impact of HIV and AIDS on both abortion and infertility counselling, and the need for supervision for those working in a counselling role with the issues raised within the book will also be offered in this chapter.

Infertility counselling

Major advances in the development of a variety of techniques and procedures since 1978 (when the first child – Louise Brown – was born as the result of in vitro fertilisation) have given childless people the opportunity to conceive, or to initiate conception, and to parent a child or children. Clinically these procedures have presented various difficulties in terms of management and successful outcomes, and the energies of those involved have been focused on overcoming these problems. The need to find causes for infertility and treatments to rectify fertility problems has been the driving force for those involved. The counselling need for those who are currently infertile, or who find the stresses of the treatments and investigations difficult or painful, has only recently been recognised and is now beginning to be addressed.

Bonnicksen, in discussing the particular procedures for IVF in this context, reflects and challenges the overall sentiment which has been the rule rather than the exception until recent years: 'To the practitioners intent on getting babies for infertile patients, the non medical implications [of freezing] are not especially interesting, important or obvious' (Bonnicksen, 1989: 40).

Incidence

In the United States, 'infertility is defined as the inability to conceive after one year of engaging in sexual intercourse without contraception (Mosher and Pratt, 1982; US Congress, Office of Technological Assessment [OTA], 1988)' (Stanton and Dunkel-Schetter, 1991: 4). The most recent indications are that about one in six couples, including those wanting a second pregnancy, seek specialist help because of their problems in conceiving (Hull, 1993). Professor Hull goes on to state that, 'amongst couples of *proven normal fertility* the highest conception rate *per monthly cycle* is 33% occurring in the first month' (Hull, 1993, emphasis in original). He makes the point that fertility in humans is not very efficient, and the large number of those seeking help is therefore unsurprising. It appears that there is no great increase in the levels of infertility, and that the numbers coming forward for help indicate the growing awareness of, and availability of, effective treatments. Mosher and Pratt observe that, 'greater numbers seeking help should not be interpreted as evidence that infertility rates are rising; infertility rates are not rising. Greater numbers seeking help are evidence that more help is available, more couples know that help is available, and a big cohort is at the age where they are most likely to use that help' (1991: 193). The 'big cohort' to which Mosher and Pratt refer is the group of people born in the years after the second World War, the 'Baby Boomers', who are now at an age where they would be seeking help for fertility problems, many having delayed having their children until their thirties.

Statistics confirm that the incidence of infertility is not increasing, but that as treatments have become more available (usually for those who can afford to pay), the number presenting has increased. The US definition of infertility indicates that between 20 and 35 per cent of couples in Britain 'take more than one year to conceive at some stage in their reproductive history' (Stanton and Dunkel-Schetter, 1991: 5). This means that the sheer numbers of those presenting are huge, taking into account the current understanding in both the US and Britain.

Definitions

The *Shorter Oxford English Dictionary* defines infertile in the following way: 'not fertile; unproductive, barren, sterile'. These words hold many negative and indeed stigmatising connotations, which have helped to form the basis of the sense of failure and worthlessness that many with a fertility problem experience.

There is no definition of fertility counselling. Any recent discussion of such a definition has generally focused on the counselling work done within an infertility unit. I believe that there is a great deal to be learned from the experience of those working within the context of abortion services. The provision of counselling and the training of counsellors within abortion agencies has been developed in Britain since the 1967 Abortion Act, and I think that an examination of the components that those working in infertility units consider important in counselling those who seek help with infertility shows that there is a high degree of compatibility between the two contexts. It is also true to say that there is a level of overlap with the work that counsellors might do within any medical setting.

> The need for counselling in medical situations is gaining increasing prominence. There is a growing awareness that if the best outcomes are to be achieved, patients need to be involved in decisions about their own treatment. (King's Fund, 1991: 2)

This report from the King's Fund Centre Counselling Committee goes on to say that, essentially, patients need to have information, support and the opportunity to deal with the life issues that any crisis may raise for them. This is the case whether a patient is confronting cancer, an unplanned or unwanted pregnancy, or infertility. 'With the primary goal of aiding infertile couples in managing their experience, practitioners began to conceptualise infertility as a major life crisis' (Stanton and Dunkel-Schetter, 1991: 8).

Various professionals have drawn on different counselling frameworks to help in the development of what might now be called fertility counselling. Mostyn, for example, says that,

> Counselling the infertile, if it is to be effective, must evolve around the body of knowledge from crisis counselling and bereavement counselling as well as the special expertise counsellors have accumulated concerning the most salient issues and stresses associated with specific infertility treatments and problems – treatment based counselling. (Mostyn, 1992: 33)

The counselling need

The emotional and psychological needs of those presenting for and undergoing these treatment procedures have been acknowledged, but have until recently been seen as secondary to the task of correcting the infertility and achieving a pregnancy. This achievement being the goal, the stress and distress experienced during the period of infertility is seen, perhaps, as being mended and healed by the pregnancy. In Britain, the Warnock Report of 1984 recognised the need to provide counselling facilities for those undergoing infertility treatments, and the Interim Licensing Authority, established in 1985, acknowledged the importance of counselling in the management of infertility.

The Third Voluntary Licensing Authority Annual Report in 1986, stated that:

> Proper counselling is possible only if space and time are available to the couple in a neutral atmosphere with a fully trained counsellor, possibly a member of the team who is not the prescribing doctor. (p. 15. Quoted from Morgan and Lee, 1991: 151)

The provision of counselling services as regulated by the Human Fertilisation and Embryology Act (HFEA) 1990, requires that four perspectives are kept in mind simultaneously. These are as follows:

> the welfare of the resulting child and other children who may be affected, the needs of infertile people, the needs of the prospective donor and the desire for assurance at societal level that the infertility services are conducted responsibly and in accordance with the provisions contained in current legislation. (King's Fund, 1991: 1)

Berg and Wilson, in a study of 104 married couples who met the definition of infertility, that is, trying to conceive for a 12-month period or more, found, 'a profile of infertility strain reflecting tension, depressive symptoms, worry, and interpersonal alienation frequently occurring among both male and female infertility patients'. They suggested the notion of 'infertility strain as a vehicle for understanding the functioning of infertile patients and to circumvent the stigmatising effects of psychiatric labels while providing appropriate intervention' (1990: 654). They expressed concern about how 'appropriate intervention' could be made available to this population, and concluded that this group (a) did not show significant psychopathology, and (b) that there was no evidence to support the notion of psychogenic infertility.

> Traditionally, proponents of the Psychogenic Infertility Model have attempted to demonstrate the existence of psychopathology, which could play an etiological role in infertility. However, studies operating from this model, which compared infertile with fertile groups on traditional measures of psychopathology, have tended to find more non significant differences than significant ones. (1990: 654)

The HFEA Code of Practice (1990) section on counselling specifies 'three distinct types of counselling' which should be made available:

> a. *implications counselling*: this aims to enable the person concerned to understand the implications of the proposed course of action for himself or herself, for his or her family and for any children born as a result;

b. *support counselling*: this aims to give emotional support at times of particular stress, e.g. when there is a failure to achieve a pregnancy;

c. *therapeutic counselling*: this aims to help people cope with the consequences of infertility and treatment, and to help them to resolve the problems which these may cause. It includes helping people to adjust their expectations and to accept their situation. (1990: 6.4.: 6.i)

The recommendation put forward by the King's Fund Centre Counselling Committee's *Report on Counselling for Regulated Infertility Treatments* (1991) is that the proper counselling which the HFEA requires should contain four components. These are:

1 Information counselling.
2 Implications counselling.
3 Support counselling.
4 Therapeutic counselling.

These components are the same as those recognised by the HFEA, with the addition of 'information counselling'. The definition of this is not clear. However, the point that is being made is that it is important, if not essential, that those who are working with fertility problems must have a working knowledge, not only of the principles and practices of counselling, but also of the procedures and techniques involved in fertility investigations, diagnosis and treatment, and an ability to impart that knowledge with sensitivity, realism and in ways that can be understood clearly by the individual or couple. It seems that counsellors who do not have this solid background in the processes involved in fertility treatments etc. find it difficult to manage the anxieties of the client(s), and the client(s) lose faith in the counsellor.

The King's Fund report (1991) goes on to say that the Committee is concerned also with the development of appropriate training programmes for infertility counsellors, and sees the inclusion of information counselling as important in laying the foundation for relevant training. The HFEA Code of Practice also states that 'No-one is obliged to accept counselling. However it is generally recognised as beneficial' (1990: 6.3:6.i).

While there has been an enormous shift in the perception of the use and effectiveness of counselling in the area of infertility and in medical settings in general, there is clearly no obligation on the part of those offering services either in infertility or in abortion clinics routinely to counsel everybody who is seeking help. 'The legal obligation is one of access to counselling; ... support counselling may be offered within centres to a variable extent but therapeutic counselling would more likely be arranged by referral to external personnel' (RCOG, 1992: 29).

The interpretation therefore of what counselling is, who should do this work and how it should be made available to those seeking help is left very much up to the service providers.

The position in the United States, in so far as counselling is concerned, is difficult to ascertain. There appears to be no statutory regulation of fertility services across the country, and certainly no statement of 'best policy' in terms of counselling practice. In her book, *In Vitro Fertilization. Building Policy from Laboratories to Legislatures*, Bonnicksen (1989) discusses the history of IVF, the new reproductive technologies and embryo research in the United States. The development of clinical practice has taken place in a political vacuum, where politicians have been unwilling to be seen to engage in the contentious issues surrounding IVF. The field of reproductive technology has become entangled with abortion policy and this has had the effect of paralysing political will.

> As a consequence of the political context of IVF, a gentlemen's agreement (in the literal as well as metaphorical sense in that most politicians and IVF practitioners are men) arose by default in which the medical community would be free to govern its own. Policy on IVF today combines self regulation by the private sector, existing laws designed to protect subjects of research, and a handful of state laws dealing directly with IVF. The initiative, however, is enjoyed primarily by the private sector, where medical groups fashion guidelines for physicians to decide what to allow and what to limit in the field of reproductive technologies. (1989: 82)

She goes on to emphasise the point that there has been no concerted effort by government to effect a policy to regulate the provision of reproductive services across the country. This leaves clinicians to develop their practice within the context of the organisations, ethical codes and laws that already exist. I understand that most clinics offer, and some impose, counselling services, often delivered by psychologists or social workers who are licensed counsellors within that particular state. It is not clear how this is evaluated and monitored or what, if any, training specific to fertility is required.

The goal of counselling

Developments in the assessment of the aetiology of infertility have led to a new understanding of the role of counselling in infertility units. Infertility is now understood to be mainly organic or physiological in causation.

> As elaborate theories about the psychodynamics of infertile people remain unconfirmed by rigorous research, and as advances in medical technology have led to improved diagnostic techniques and a better understanding of reproductive physiology, a diagnosis can now be

established for more than 90 per cent of infertile cases (Mazor, 1984: p. 24). In the remaining 10 per cent, the difficulty in obtaining an accurate diagnosis may be attributed to inadequate technology. (Shapiro, 1988: 7)

This does not necessarily mean, however, that there may not be a negative feedback loop within the individual or couple which occurs, and which *may* have its own impact on fertility. Thus the stress of the infertility diagnosis, investigations and treatments may negatively impact on the person's chances of conception. The physiological connections between stress and infertility are little understood and more research is needed in this area. What is clear is, that however well meant, instructions to 'go away for a holiday and relax', do nothing to reduce a couple's stress, especially if they do not have a sense of control about it, and often gives the message that their current infertility is 'self induced' in some way.

In their book *Infertility. Perspectives from Stress and Coping Research*, Stanton and Dunkel-Schetter have this to say about the impact of stress:

> Finding an anatomical, physiological, or neuroendocrinological cause for infertility does not preclude the possibility that psychological factors also contribute. In particular, several researchers have discussed the mechanisms whereby stress may affect spermatogenesis and ovulation (Domar and Seibal, 1990; Edelman and Golombok, 1989; Giblin, Poland, Moghissi, Ager and Olson, 1988; Harrison, Calla and Hennessey, 1987; Seibal and Taymor, 1982). Thus, stress is a possible interactive etiologic factor. (1991: 7)

The goal of the counsellor, therefore, has changed from one in which she or he is aiming to uncover the unconscious conflicts impeding conception, and thus allowing a pregnancy to occur, to that of stress reduction, support and working with the impact of the processes and procedures as they arise.

In one US study carried out on a population of 185 couples in Michigan, the authors suggest, 'that attempts by health care providers to increase patient's sense of control, optimism (within realistic limits), and social support should reduce stress' (Abbey et al., 1992: 57;122). This is, I believe, the primary aim in the work of the infertility counsellor. If there are indications that the fertility issues have unlocked deeper traumas, or difficulties, then decisions about referral to appropriate therapy may need to be made.

Abortion counselling

Counselling women and couples who are seeking a termination of pregnancy involves giving clear information, contains elements of crisis counselling and bereavement counselling, as well as the ability on the part of the counsellor to make a judgement as to whether the client(s) may need referral to an external source for further help to deal with the issues that this crisis may have raised for them. This is similar, at a process level, to the point made above about the work of a counsellor in an infertility unit. For the purpose of this discussion, abortion is meant to signify a termination of a pregnancy, as distinct from a miscarriage or spontaneous abortion.

Incidence

In England and Wales, in 1992, the last year for which statistics are available, the Office of Population Censuses and Surveys gives the figure for the total number of legal abortions as 172,063. This is inclusive of both the resident and non-resident figures. The total number of abortions for resident women was 160,495. These figures represent a slight decrease of 4.2 per cent and 4.1 per cent respectively, and for the resident women, aged between 14 and 49 years, a rate of 12.51 TOPs (terminations of pregnancy) per 1000 women (OPCS, 1992). There has been little change in the proportion of women seeking abortion since the introduction of the 1967 Abortion Act, and in an article published in the *British Medical Journal*, David Paintin, then a Research Fellow at St Mary's Hospital, London, makes this observation:

> The lack of change in the proportion of pregnancies ending in legal abortion suggests that the behavioural factors that lead to unwanted conception and abortion are intrinsic to our society and that easy availability is not a primary factor in the decision concerning abortion. (1992: 967)

This is an important point, since those who oppose abortion seem to believe that should abortion become more 'freely' available, there would be a marked increase in the numbers of women who choose legal abortion, and that any 'loosening' of the restrictions that pertain to abortion in England and Wales should therefore be opposed. His statement would also seem to have some relevance when the position in the United States is considered. The abortion rates in the United States, as in England and Wales, have stayed at a consistent level, with a slight decrease in the past decade.

> Since 1980, the national number (and rate) of abortions has remained relatively stable, with only small (<5%) year-to-year fluctuations.

However, since 1984 the national abortion rate has declined. In 1990, the abortion ratio was the lowest recorded since 1977. (MMWR, 1993: 29)

In both the United States and in England and Wales the vast majority of legal abortions were performed before the 13th week of pregnancy. In the United States this was 87 per cent in 1990 (MMWR, 1993), and in England and Wales the percentage was 88 per cent in 1991 (Family Planning Association, 1994a).

The legal position: United States
In the United States the major piece of legislation that defines the position of abortion is *Roe* v. *Wade*. This was the 1973 Supreme Court decision that first recognised the woman's right to decide to terminate her pregnancy (Mariner, 1992: 1556). This decision has been under attack ever since, much as the 1967 Abortion Act in Britain (excluding Northern Ireland) has been, and there have been some restrictions placed on this right to abortion in the United States. The conflicts surrounding the understanding and interpretation of this right are deeply felt and hotly argued. At the heart of this debate in the United States is the conflict between the constitutional rights of the woman to 'be free to develop and believe in her own idea of life itself and define her own conception of the Good' (Mariner, 1992: 1557). She goes on to quote the US Supreme Court's decision in *Planned Parenthood of Southeastern Pennsylvania* v. *Casey* in which the judges

> eloquently defend constitutional protection of the right to make intimate decisions like continuing or ending a pregnancy. At the same time, they permit the state to try to persuade pregnant women not to have abortions and to make abortion harder to obtain and more costly, as long as the state's methods do not create an 'undue burden' on the decision (Mariner, 1992: 1556)

The ambivalence that this case shows seems to exemplify the tension that the 'right to abortion' creates between not only the right to the self determination by the woman over her body and her life, and the 'right to life' of the foetus, but also the tension between the responsibilities of the individual towards herself and her family and the responsibilities of the state towards its citizens (as yet unborn?).

The legal position: Britain
This is defined by the Abortion Act 1967 Amended 1990 (see Appendices). There is a very clear description of the provisions of this Act, its link with the Human Fertilisation and Embryology Act

1990, and the changes that have been made to it as a result of the link with the 1990 Act, in Morgan and Lee's book on the Human Fertilisation and Embryology Act 1990, subtitled *Abortion and Embryo Research, The New Law.* An important change to note is the severance of the link that applied previously with the Infant Life (Preservation) Act 1929.

Essentially, any woman who is considering a decision to terminate her pregnancy, whether as a result of her social, economic, personal, family or medical circumstances, must have the consent of two medical practitioners before the abortion may be performed. The clauses in the Abortion Act 1967 as amended by the HFE Act 1990 under which she can do this and to which the two doctors must conform are as follows:

(a)   that the pregnancy has not exceeded its 24th week and that the continuance of the pregnancy would involve risk to the life of the pregnant woman, or of injury to the physical or mental health of the pregnant woman or any existing children of her family, greater than if the pregnancy were terminated; or

(b)   that the termination is necessary to prevent grave permanent injury to the physical or mental health of the pregnant woman; or

(c)   that the continuance of the pregnancy would involve risk to the life of the pregnant woman, greater than if the pregnancy were terminated; or

(d)   that there is a substantial risk that if the child were born it would suffer from such physical or mental abnormalities as to be seriously handicapped.

Thus, it is clear that the procedures for a woman to have a legal termination of her pregnancy are grounded not only in the medical aspects, but are based in the need to adhere to the law of abortion. When a woman presents for consideration of an abortion, therefore, she is entering a legal process, and any counselling which is offered takes place within that context. So, for example, a counsellor *cannot* offer the woman complete reassurance that her pregnancy will be terminated, since until she has had the consent of the two medical practitioners who agree under which clause she is entitled to terminate her pregnancy, it is not a certainty that she can have it done. In some cases this causes great anxiety to the woman, and she may need to see the doctors before she can take advantage of any counselling that is offered to her.

There is no requirement on the part of health authorities to provide abortion services, and abortion provision is not consistent across the country. In some areas, the service may be relatively available through the health service, and in other areas there will be little provision and women will either have to pay for a legal termination in the private sector, or non-profit-making charity sector, as well as possibly having to travel some distance to get to a private clinic. Therefore a counsellor working in the private or non-profit-making charity sector (where fees are charged at cost) may be confronted with a woman who has had to overcome several obstacles in her search to terminate her pregnancy and may be angry and distressed as a result of these factors, as well as or even rather than as a result of the situation in which she is considering an abortion. Equally, a counsellor working within health service provision, may be working with women who have fewer economic resources, and who could not afford to have a private abortion. This may mean that her anxiety about obtaining a free abortion could affect how she presents and whether she expresses any ambivalence, which she may feel could affect her chances of getting an abortion. This dynamic may operate in any context, since as noted above, there is the requirement to have two medical practitioners agree to the abortion. Thus women may hide anything which they believe may jeopardise their chances.

There have been various challenges to the 1967 Abortion Act over the years, and clearly these challenges will continue. However, there seems to be a general understanding that people feel that the current system works quite well. Additionally, there is evidence that attitudes towards abortion, and abortion provision have liberalised over the past 10–15 years. In a factsheet on the legal and ethical issues surrounding abortion, the Family Planning Association (1994b) quote the British Social Attitudes Survey, in which it was shown that 95 per cent of people in 1989 as opposed to 87 per cent in 1983, felt that abortion should be allowed when the woman's health was endangered. This trend was consistent when other questions, such as the economic situation of the woman and her family, and the woman's own choice was considered. This trend is reflected in the medical profession also. 'A national survey of consultant gynaecologists in 1989 found that 73% believed that a woman should have the right to choose abortion' (Paintin, 1992: 968). This survey, carried out by Savage and Francome (1989), also showed that 87 per cent of consultant gynaecologists felt that the Royal College of Obstetricians and Gynaecologists had been right to oppose one of the more recent challenges to the Abortion Act, the Alton Bill.

It is within this context of growing understanding and acceptance of the need for abortion, as well as the challenges and attacks on abortion, that the counsellor works with the woman who is considering this course of action. Both will be affected by the latest debates, the most recent headlines, as well as their personal beliefs and prejudices. It is the counsellor's role to take account of the context, and create an environment in which the woman can make decisions in the light of her circumstances, beliefs and feelings.

When considering the overall model of fertility counselling as presented by the King's Fund Committee and discussed earlier in this chapter, it is possible, taking each of the components in turn, to make clear comparisons with the counselling models that have operated within the context of abortion counselling for many years.

Information counselling
For many women, and their partners, much of their anxiety or apprehension about having an abortion is to do with not knowing what happens, not just in an abortion operation, but also in the process that the woman must enter in order to get an abortion. One of the roles that a counsellor takes when working with this client group is that of information giver. Thus, the counsellor must know about the procedures for termination of pregnancy at various stages of pregnancy, as well as the kind and impact of anaesthetics used, at least in general terms. The counsellor must also be familiar with different contraceptive methods, and be able to discuss the impact of these methods on the woman or couple, so that she or they can make a choice that will be appropriate for them. The counsellor needs also to know the laws and regulations that bind and surround abortion, and be able to explain these to the client as necessary. The effect of giving information to a woman in this situation can be powerful indeed in enabling her to make informed choices within a social, cultural, legal as well as an emotional context. The reduction of anxiety is common where the woman has been presented with clear, understandable information, and where she has been engaged in the process of making judgements for herself as to her best course of action.

Implications counselling
Much of the work that a counsellor does in an abortion service is helping the woman and, as appropriate, her husband, partner or parent(s), to look at, explore the feelings around, and understand the significance of her pregnancy and the decision to have an abortion. Questions such as, 'What would be the situation if you were to continue the pregnancy?' and 'How do you think you might feel after a termination of the pregnancy?', are used by the

counsellor in an attempt to begin the process of helping the client understand for herself the implications of her decisions.

Support counselling

This, in a sense, is a movement on from implications counselling, and begins the process of helping the client, both in the fertility unit and the abortion clinic, to examine her needs within the decisions that she is making. What does she need in order for her to feel as comfortable as possible with her decision? What can the counsellor offer in terms of understanding, role play practice, encouragement, that may enable the client to feel supported through the process?

Therapeutic counselling

The counsellor in either the fertility unit or the abortion clinic must be able to assess the needs of the client(s), to ensure as far as possible that there is no significant disturbance or deeper distress, which the stress or significance of their situation has activated. It is not always possible or appropriate for the counsellor within the unit to provide the therapeutic counselling personally, and the counsellor's role is to assess the need and to ensure that a referral is available.

Therapeutic counselling would involve the work of bringing into conscious awareness the depth of the distress and the familiar patterns of behaviour and of feeling which the client is struggling with, and which she or he has been keeping at a pre- or sub-conscious level of awareness. The need for this would be indicated by the inability of the client to make decisions, serious and intransigent ambivalence about various beliefs or courses of action. Manifestations of this could be an inability on the part of clients to believe that they have any control over the situation; 'over-the-top' anger about their position, indicating unresolved 'old' anger; or deep and long lasting depression. These responses may need further work with the counsellor, if it can be done within the context of the clinic, or referral to a therapist.

The motivation to form a model of counselling for fertility problems has raised the issues of what counselling in this context should consist of, and has helped to give shape to the work that the abortion counsellor has been doing over many years. The modalities that other counselling contexts offer, such as crisis counselling, bereavement counselling and stress counselling, have underpinned the development of a discrete 'off-shoot' or subsidiary of counselling, called fertility counselling. Fertility counselling includes both counselling those who are infertile and those who have an unplanned or unwanted pregnancy.

HIV and AIDS: impact on fertility counselling

It is impossible to consider counselling for infertility or about abortion, without reference to HIV infection and AIDS. There has been a growing awareness and understanding within the client groups about the impact of HIV and AIDS on sexual activity and potential life style. The issues break down into three broad areas. First, the professionals' understanding, and safety; secondly, the client's awareness, concerns and safety; and thirdly, concerns for the future of any child born as the result of assisted conception techniques.

For some women considering termination of pregnancy, the circumstances in which they conceived, a brief sexual encounter, a rape, or where they find that a partner is HIV positive, may have left them vulnerable to HIV infection. This needs to be taken into account within the context of the counselling interview. The knowledge of their vulnerability to the risk of HIV infection may be one of the reasons for which a termination of pregnancy is sought. Any HIV testing may be done within the agency, although it is often done through local Genito-Urinary Medicine Departments, where full pre- and post-HIV test counselling is available, and staff are properly trained for the work. Counsellors need to have a working knowledge of HIV infection and AIDS to be able to offer appropriate help and referral.

Those who are currently infertile may not consider that HIV and AIDS concerns them directly. Some are anxious about the HIV status of donors, and will need what reassurance is realistic about the safety of the donor screening procedures. HIV testing counselling should be available and routine for all donors. This is probably most easily incorporated into the general counselling for donors, although it may be offered by the doctor, nurse or local HIV testing unit staff, as well as the counsellor.

There are some clinics which routinely screen the infertile couple or individual for HIV infection. This is done, at least in Britain, to comply with a broad interpretation of the HFEA's desire that the best interest of the child be a paramount consideration in any decision to treat. In one unit, for example, their 'independent Ethics Committee believe that it is in the best interests of the child . . . [and] . . . will continue to screen routinely' (personal communication: P. Brinsden, 1994). In this case, 'the best interests of the child' seems to include the desire to ensure that the child has the best chance of having its parent(s) around for most of its early life, and for it not to have to manage the possible chronic illness of one (or both) of its parents. Another unit does not test the couple, but like many units will 'not offer treatment to women who are either the partners of HIV positive men or who are HIV positive themselves' (personal communication: S. Cooke, 1994). This all opens the debate about the 'appropriateness' of offering fertility treatment to those with any kind of disability or impairment. In Britain the situation is unclear, with some units willing to treat client groups with some disability or chronic condition, including treating HIV positive people, and some not.

The legal position has not so far been tested. However, it seems that in Britain 'If IVF succeeds the doctors could incur liability to the HIV positive mother in negligence if they fail to inform her of the risk that the pregnancy may accelerate the progress of the disease' (Doyle and Delany, 1991: 1447). As far as the liability of the doctor to the child is concerned, 'According to the Congenital Disabilities (Civil Liability) Act 1976 as amended by the Human Fertilisation and Embryology Act 1990, a child born disabled can sue whoever has negligently caused the disability . . . and section 44 of the Human Fertilisation and Embryology Act 1990 extends liability to cover negligent acts done in the course of infertility treatments' (Doyle and Delany, 1991: 1447–8).

Referral for post-HIV counselling, should the result be positive, is a matter for the individual units and should take into account the availability of local resources. The Human Fertilisation and Embryology Authority do not, in fact, insist upon HIV testing for couples seeking treatment, but do for those who will be donating their sperm or their eggs.

Most units have evolved a policy about HIV testing, who does it and what its purpose is with regard to both the donors and the clients. This is not entirely consistent and will no doubt change further over time, as understanding of HIV and AIDS grows and HIV testing procedures develop.

Adoption

Not all those who are infertile will choose adoption as their first option to create a family. In fact, for many, there will seem little point in attempting the adoption route, since by the time they have discovered there is a fertility problem they will already be ineligible in age terms as adoptive parents, at least for adopting a small baby. The hope held out to those who have a fertility problem to have a biologically linked child, or a child where the parents have been involved throughout conception, pregnancy and delivery, means that many prospective adopters are now waiting until all possibilities have been pursued before considering adoption. The other aspect of the situation with regard to adoption is the shortage of small babies for adoption. This is a result of two major factors. First, many of those women who might once have given up their child for adoption are choosing now to have an abortion, rather than go through the pain of carrying a child to term and then having it adopted. Secondly, there seems to be less stigma attached to single motherhood, and many women are choosing to keep their babies and raise them themselves.

However, almost all those who choose adoption will do so because they are infertile or are unwilling to risk having a child that is genetically damaged in some way. Thus adoption workers often have to work with the feelings that the couple have about their failed fertility treatments, and the end of their quest for a biologically linked child. Some couples who are considering adoption find themselves in a dilemma about what to say to adoption agencies, since many agencies stipulate that any couple presenting for consideration as adoptive parents must have 'come to terms with their infertility'. This seems to mean that such couples should have ended any fertility treatment and adjusted to the loss of a child through such means. However, as new advances are made in sperm retrieval, or fertilization techniques, such as sub-zonal insemination (SUZI) or intra-cytoplasmic sperm injection (ICSI), these couples, who may have come to 'the end of the road', find that six months later the road suddenly opens up in front of them again. This can make it very hard for a couple to end fertility treatment permanently, and thus become eligible for adoption lists.

The concerns of adoption agencies are different from the concerns of those who offer couples fertility treatment. Adoption agencies have children whom they wish to place appropriately and thus wish to assess suitability in prospective adopters. As part of this they are concerned to ensure that couples are aware of the particular differences and issues involved in being adoptive parents. In a publication from the British Agencies for Adoption and Fostering, *The Role of Infertility in Adoption*, the following statement is made in the introduction:

> Not all infertile couples decide to try to form a family by adoption. When they do, it becomes important to understand the psychological impact of the infertility upon the couple and their relationship with each other, and upon their motivation for adoption and their expectations of and attitudes to the adopted child. (Brebner et al., 1985: 5)

There seems to be some validity in ensuring as far as possible that couples are aware that forming a family by adoption entails differences in attitudes and understanding, which may not have been part of their original decision to form a family by 'normal' means. There seems to be a clear policy in adoption work that couples must have made this adjustment. However, the assessment of this understanding and acceptance of the differences by the prospective adoptive parents seems to be vague and open to prejudice and bias on the part of the assessors.

> The self concepts of the persons who experience infertility are (thus) reorganised around issues other than fertility if the couple is to make a good adjustment. If this adaptation is not made, the couple is not only less successful in handling the crisis [of adoption], but also less likely to successfully master subsequent developmental stages and tasks of the family life cycle. (le Pere, 1988: 78)

However, the process of adjusting to the loss of a biologically linked child is an important one, and recognising that this process is complete may be difficult. As with any loss there will always be moments when the sense of loss is felt quite acutely again, perhaps years later, and in the case of those who have adopted, this may be when their adopted child produces their 'own' child, for example. 'If the infertile couple can successfully mourn their loss, they may be able to consider alternatives to parenthood' (le Pere, 1988: 78). The question of how an adequate adjustment to this loss is made, and further, is assessed, is particularly difficult.

The concept of an 'adoption identity' is one which appears in the literature on adoption. This is where an adjustment has been made to the notion of forming a family by adoption and in some texts there is a plea on the part of social work agencies for those involved in fertility work to consider the possibility of what adoption means more carefully.

> Doctors are preoccupied with the infertile patient, where the right to conceive is paramount. Yet as soon as infertility proves untreatable, or even earlier if adoption is being discussed as one possible solution, the doctor should first and foremost keep in mind the needs and rights of adopted children and the fact that these are invested in a social work agency. Unless doctors understand the need for this change in direction, and indeed the change in their role, it may prove more difficult to help the prospective adoptive parents towards their new adoption identity. (Brebner et al., 1985: 71–2)

The desire to protect the interests of the child that has been the cornerstone of adoption policy in England and Wales has been transferred to form some of the thinking that has gone into the formulation of the legal framework for the regulation of fertility treatment and the licensing of clinics in Britain. This contribution from the adoption experience has been helpful as well as timely.

Genetic counselling

The connections between genetic counselling and infertility counselling may seem to be tenuous. They are, however, worthy of some short comment and exploration.

Those couples who face the loss of their child through genetic disease, or are placed in the position of making a choice between not having a child and risking having a child with possibly severe disability, may choose to use donated gametes to overcome their difficulty. In this instance the grief and loss issues may be similar to those experienced by those who face infertility. Couples react to an unfavourable diagnosis of a genetic problem in much the same way as when a diagnosis of a fertility problem is given, as described in Chapter 2. That is to say, with shock, denial and anger, and with consequent sadness and depression. However, these couples are not infertile, and may already have an affected child or children.

More and more couples are looking to the work that has been done in IVF and micro-manipulation to help them ensure that the children they have are free of the genetic defect: 'in December 1988 Dr Robert Winston, Professor of Fertility Studies at the Hammersmith Hospital London, announced a programme to carry out genetic screening of embryos to detect disabling conditions' (Walby and Symons, 1990: 107). Thus couples will go through 'fertility treatment', have IVF, the fertilised eggs will be examined for the abnormality, and only those fertilised eggs that are clear of the genetic problem will be replaced. The success of this is no more certain for this client population than it is for those who seek fertility treatment to overcome infertility. However, there are implications for the counselling aspect of this work. Couples may already be dealing with the loss of a child, either through the genetic condition itself, or because they have chosen to abort an affected foetus. 'Psychological trauma is implicit in the loss of a desired pregnancy; thus the reaction to selective abortion is closely akin to the grief response to perinatal death' (Blumberg, 1984: 211). Couples may be preparing to deal with the death of their child. Thus the work of the counsellor in this situation may be more directed at the grief aspects and active management of them. It is not essential for the infertility counsellor to have an in depth knowledge of the genetic conditions which a couple may present. However, counsellors may need to familiarise themselves with the main aspects of the genetic problem. The focus of any work would ordinarily be on the loss of the wanted child, since most parents will, even if there is an affected child, experience loss and possibly anger that the child is not what they ideally have wanted. 'The birth of a defective child also may be viewed as a pregnancy loss, since the parents are deprived of the idealised, healthy child who had been expected' (Blumberg, 1984: 203–4). This work would be followed by focusing on the aspects of fertility treatments that are appropriate and the choices that the couple need to make about these.

Supervision

The supervision of counsellors who work with fertility issues may be done through a variety of mechanisms. Some may have supervision within the team that they work with in the unit. Others may use supervision that they find outside that context. What supervision means is not uniformly understood, and I will attempt briefly to put a case for the appropriate supervision of fertility counsellors.

Supervision is a process through which the counsellor gains greater understanding of the way in which she or he works with the clients/patients, how the work may be affected by personal responses to the situation, how this may be positively managed and how the counsellor may become more effective in her or his inter-actions with the client group. It is not helpful to think of supervision as being told what to do. The work that counsellors do with those who have fertility problems raises all kinds of questions about what is 'normal', about family, sex, death and loss, relation-ships, parenting and children. These are fundamentals in our society, people feel strongly about them and the work challenges us to examine our assumptions, prejudices and values about these issues. The counsellor, in particular, must have a place in which she or he can explore feelings about these, in order to be truly able to be available to the clients/patients, in a way which will facilitate them to make the choices that they are faced with. Team meetings are helpful, but they are not enough to help the counsellor to confront and challenge her or his work, and to become more effective.

Peer supervision is also helpful, although it is essential that any such sessions are focused on supervision and do not become a place to air grievances and complain about the system. It is probably appropriate for supervision to be supplied by those who have an understanding of the issues involved in the work, and the specifics of working in an area which is at the forefront of medical tech-nology and which challenges what are seen as 'basic' assumptions in our society. The British Infertility Counselling Association offers the only resource that I am aware of, both to clients/patients in their search for independent counsellors, but also to counsellors who wish to get supervision within this context. I believe that it is essential for those who work with fertility issues to receive supervision from those who themselves are clinically experienced in this area. There is a clear need for the development of supervision training to provide appropriate support to those who are working at the forefront of fertility counselling.

2

Overview of the Counselling Model for Working with Fertility Problems

In this chapter I want to offer a way of exploring and understanding the process of counselling people who have a fertility problem. There are four models that I wish to introduce, and three of these may already be familiar to many helping professionals. For this reason, I will not describe them in full detail, but show how they may be integrated to form a framework that I have found useful as a way of understanding the work. The fourth model is one that I have developed to help my own understanding of work with infertile people within the context of an infertility unit.

The first two models are of grief counselling and therapy: one from the work of Dr Elisabeth Kubler-Ross, focused on those who are in the process of dying, and the other from J. William Worden's analysis of the tasks of mourning. The relevance of using these grief and bereavement counselling frameworks when working with those who undergo the process of infertility diagnosis and treatment is pointed out by Nancy Adler, who says,

> The experience of infertility is potentially one of the most painful events of life to which people must adjust. It is a complex experience affecting the woman, the man, and the couple. It is fraught with uncertainty and can lead to alternating hope and despair. It brings people into contact with the leading edge of biomedical technology, where uncertainties abound and procedures are costly, painful and intrusive. Multiple losses can result. (1991: ix)

The third model is Gerard Egan's three-stage model of counselling. I have found this model immensely useful in framing the content of particular sessions with clients in working with almost any aspect of their fertility issue, and I will describe it later in this chapter.

The fourth model, which I have developed myself for working with those who have a fertility problem, will be discussed fully later in this chapter.

Kubler-Ross's grief counselling model

Kubler-Ross (1973) has developed the notion of 'stages' as a way of formulating the grief process.

Stage 1   Denial and Isolation
The realisation that there is a problem in conceiving may dawn slowly upon the infertile person. There may be a reluctance to seek medical help for fear of finding that there is a problem. This denial may be operating for some time before it is clearly understood that there is any difficulty.

Some may experience shock and disbelief when they hear the results of tests confirming sub-fertility (that is, low fertility, such as oligospermia, or ovulation problems) or infertility. In this case, denial can take the form of seeking other opinions, or wanting to believe that the test results are wrong or have been mistaken for someone else's. Other people may have always known that they are infertile, for example, women who have Turner's Syndrome, a congenital abnormality where the female is born without functioning ovaries. Here, they may have denied the importance of this to themselves or to others. Spouses or partners may also have denied, at the beginning of a relationship, the significance of infertility for them. This may make it particularly difficult for them later to address their desire for children and can cause considerable distress within the relationship.

Elements of denial may re-emerge in the process of infertility treatments when, for example, an IVF attempt does not result in conception. The person or couple may deny the effect of this 'failure' on them.

Many people are unable or unwilling to share their growing fears and concerns with family, friends or sometimes with their spouse, and withdrawal from this network of potential support is a common feature with many couples. They may feel that the diagnosis is a stigma, which they cannot, out of shame and embarrassment, share with anyone. There is often a feeling that others cannot understand, and a growing sense of isolation.

Case example

Zoe is married to John, and they have wanted to have a child for the past four years. She has had one pregnancy which ended in an early miscarriage. It is unclear what the cause of their fertility problem is. Zoe works in the public sector and has a close and loving relationship with her husband, which has nevertheless been put under some pressure as a result of their difficulties in conceiving. Zoe's family are also understanding, although generally fairly reserved. Zoe is seen on her own throughout the counselling process. This is important in that it partly expresses her need and desire to have time for herself to work her feelings and thoughts through, and partly indicates her sense of 'this is my fault and my problem, so I must deal with it by myself'. This 'claim to blame', with its consequent decision to seek help alone rather than with the partner or husband, is not uncommon within this client population. It may indicate a need for control which is perceived as harder to maintain if the spouse is included in the counselling. I will be following Zoe's story, and the processes through which she passes, in Chapters 4 and 5.

> Zoe: That's the hardest, one of the hardest parts [*weeping*], I'm so angry with them, I *am* angry with them, and, this sounds so pathetic, but I looked through my address book, John was away, and I felt so desperate, and I thought I've just got to speak to someone, just to calm down, and I couldn't find anybody that I could phone, there wasn't really anybody because all of them have got children now, and I knew they wouldn't understand anyway, and I just felt so alone.

As time has gone on, this woman has felt more and more that those around her have been unable or unwilling to maintain support and encouragement for her and she feels angry, betrayed and isolated by this.

> It is difficult for networks to remain mobilised to provide specific support functions when stressors last for years, as many chronic stressors do. Thus, over time, support providers may become less responsive to signs that support is required. (Abbey et al., 1991: 64)

Zoe also speaks of her intense anger and it is worthwhile to note that here her anger is appearing in the Denial and Isolation phase in Kubler-Ross's model. Anger may be present in any of the phases, however, and not only in the Anger phase. There may also be withdrawal from the spouse or partner, perhaps especially if there has been little discussion of the problems, and if one of the couple feels more involved or apparently has more invested in having a child than the other.

Stage 2   Anger
This is shown by those who are managing their infertility in many ways. Commonly, however, there is hostility towards family, friends and partners. Often people express their anger in a 'righteous' way

by pointing out faults in others' parenting or care during pregnancy. For example, someone might say, 'Look at her, she's smoking, she can't care about her child, *I* wouldn't do that. It's not fair, I would be a much better mother!' Anger may be expressed in a blaming way. A spouse or partner may say, 'It's her fault, she should have agreed to have a child straight away, not worry about her career so much!'

Consider this counselling interview with Zoe:

> *Zoe*: After this phone call with this friend, and I just felt so angry, really angry, and I'm upset about being so angry, really out of control, and it's just a bit frightening.
> *Counsellor*: Tell me about the anger.
> *Zoe*: I phoned up this other friend, and she just, well she said that she was pregnant, and she was thinking about having an abortion, and she was very blasé about it, and I'd spoken to her already about what had happened to me and she just seemed like she didn't take any of that into account, she just seemed really blasé, talking about having an abortion and then she decided not to, so I said 'Oh I'm really pleased for you' and I said 'I have to say it seems a little bit unfair, I've been trying for three and a half years, and you didn't even want this, and now you've got pregnant,' and she said 'well, I think the problem with you is you're too thin', and just started to say 'it's your diet or something', and I just went mad, I just said 'Fuck off', and it just came, I was just so angry with her.

For Zoe, the sense of being out of control of her situation, her feeling that others could not or would not understand and then a friend telling her that the problem was in a way her fault, led to an explosion of anger that she experienced as terrifying, both in its intensity and in the fact of its being so uncharacteristic in Zoe's perception of who she is. The work for the counsellor here is in containing and validating her anger, and allowing her to express it safely and appropriately.

Anger may be directed also towards those in clinic services. This can take the form of expressions of dissatisfaction with the service provided, such as surgery or appointments being scheduled at inconvenient times. There may be complaints about the cost of treatment, or not seeing the consultant on each visit. It is important for the staff in infertility units to be aware that this is relatively common and for them to respond sensitively. Clients' fear and anger at their apparent loss of control in such situations is understandable and needs to be contained. Clients should be encouraged to take as much charge of their treatment as they can. It is important that clients know the limits of the unit's work and that staff should not be afraid to say 'no' to unreasonable demands or behaviour, even if it is possible that the person could respond angrily. The knowledge that the clinic staff know the limits of their work and of the system will allow clients to feel more secure in what for them is a difficult and painful situation.

Stage 3   Bargaining

Bargaining is the stage at which the person attempts, by various means, to exert control over the situation. Bargaining is a process which can take the form of attempting to 'trade' one scenario for another, and can be manifested in a variety of ways. For those couples who may be some way into the long process of investigations and treatments, there often comes a time where their goals apparently shift considerably. At this point the infertile person may entertain the childlike notion that if they demand less and behave more 'acceptably', then 'they' (God, or some other omnipotent being, possibly with the face of a clinic doctor), will allow them to have a child. So, for the infertile person this can take the form of greater compliance with the clinic programmes. They may well say to themselves, or to others, 'if only I could just conceive, then I'd know that it was possible. I'd feel a "real woman". I could cope much better even if the pregnancy didn't come to term.' Alternatively the bargain may be, 'If I could have just one child then I promise that I'll be the best parent ever'. However, this often changes if the original wish 'comes true'. The couple want not just to conceive but to carry the child to term, they do not want just one child, they want two or three.

Stage 4   Depression

Over time, many couples find that they begin to despair of achieving their goal of having their own biological child. The infertile person may become depressed. This can feel quite over-whelming as they face the possibility that the child for which they have striven may never be theirs.

> *Zoe*: [*sigh*] I just wish . . . I think I thought it would start to get easier, but it just doesn't. Two and a half years. I know it's probably such a short time compared to other people, but it seems such a long time, I would have thought that it would have started to get easier. I just feel that I need to cry and cry and cry, I seem to cry really easily.

This sense of despair may be accompanied by an increase in anxiety and heightened tension, as the couple confront their fears associated with childlessness.

Zoe: I've lost interest in everything ... the future feels so out of control, I don't know what to do. I get out of breath and everything. It frightens me . . . .

Counsellor: It seems difficult to see a future and you feel scared and panicky?

Zoe: Yes, that's it.

For this woman the feelings associated with loss of control over her fertility had come to the forefront after she had completed an important professional project. In essence, she had held back these feelings, and was only now able to confront them and begin to recognise and deal with them.

It is important to distinguish between sadness as a healthy response to a major shift in one's self image and sense of one's place in the world, which requires recognition, time and understanding to work through, and the depression that develops into a more sustained response, which will need more long-term management to resolve. I will discuss this issue of 'stuck' grief further in Chapter 4.

The losses attached to childlessness may include loss of faith, loss of power, loss of dreams of the future and loss of sexual function and intimacy. Commonly for the man there is the loss of the image of himself as 'virile', and for the woman a view of herself as 'feminine'. This is often discussed in terms of a sense of failure. The couple feel that they have failed in a basic task, that is, to have a family.

Stage 5   Acceptance
This can be defined as the point at which the person has accepted the reality of the loss and is then able to put energy into the present and is planning for the future. I believe that this sense of acceptance may emerge at any stage of the infertility treatment or management process. It may become apparent in different ways and at different times. Couples may come to accept that they will never have a child and feel able and even eager to move forward to a new life without children. In other ways, the infertile man or woman may come to an acceptance of their personal infertility, and feel ready to consider the option of donated sperm or ova to help them to have a child within their relationship. The 'fertile' partner in the relationship will need to accept that she or he will not have the imagined child of the relationship, and be ready to incorporate a different way of creating a family, or a different 'child free' future. At these times, the person or couple will have grieved the loss of their fertility as well as the loss of their own biological child. They will be prepared to move on with renewed energy to the acceptance of a child through adoption

or gamete donation. Acceptance may be indicated by a positive decision not to begin or to continue treatment, or to take up a treatment option that previously had been unacceptable to them.

Case example

James and Jenny had been married for a number of years and had built good careers and a secure financial base. This they had done with a carefully considered view that they wanted to have a family in the best circumstances that they could provide. After two years of 'trying' they discovered that James was azoospermic, that is, he had no sperm at all. This news devastated them both. However, Jenny moved relatively quickly through her own shock and sadness and decided that she was ready to proceed with donor insemination (DI). She had grieved and accepted that she would be unable to have a joint biological child with James. She was excited and energised by the possibility of DI and was eager to move ahead with this. She was concerned, but not overly so, about the procedures involved, and wanted information about these. However she was very clear within herself that she would be able to accept, love and raise a child conceived in this way.

For James this process took much longer. He found it hard to reconcile his image of himself as a happy-go-lucky man, in charge of his life, with this person, who, in his view, was not now whole. He found it difficult to consider the option of Jenny having DI, as he thought that it was like adultery, and felt disgusted by this. He became depressed and thought constantly about his infertility. He also believed that in some way if this was what fate or God had decided he must face, then he should not take the 'easy way out'.

Counselling consisted of encouraging him to evaluate his beliefs in the light of his experience, to express his pain, his anger and his grief at the loss of his fertility, the loss of his sense of himself as complete and in charge of his life, and at the loss of his genetic child/ren. In this way he felt able to take greater control over his life, and to consider the choices that were open to him in a more informed way. He stopped thinking constantly about his infertility, became less depressed and more active in the decisions which they as a couple needed to make.

It needs to be understood that not all people are able to proceed through these stages to a peaceful conclusion. There will be many who do not make these transitions, and those also who are unwilling to acknowledge at any stage the reality of their situation and stay in denial until the choices are removed from them, by time, financial constraints, the medical profession or other circumstances. It is also important to note that these stages are guidelines only and many may apparently skip stages, or revert to previous feelings and behaviours that are seen to be a part of earlier stages, at any time during this process.

J. William Worden's grief counselling model

The second model is taken from J. William Worden's work (1991) on grief counselling and grief therapy, in which he outlines four *tasks of grieving*. Infertility may be conceptualised in this way, and is perhaps all the more painful, since the loss is an unseen one. Nonetheless, it is a loss that must be grieved.

Task 1   To accept the reality of the loss

Worden argues that it is necessary for the grieving process that the loss is fully acknowledged, and says that denial of the loss may take many forms, including total denial. This is not unusual for short periods of time, but may indicate that the person is stuck in the inability to acknowledge the reality of the loss. Other forms of denial may be shown by discounting the significance of the loss.

The infertile person may search for another diagnosis, or may keep a 'baby fund', possibly including clothes, toys, nursery and so on, or may be unable to let go of a scan picture of the implanted embryo, after an IVF attempt, carrying it everywhere with them.

Task 2   To work through the pain of the grief

Worden makes the point that, 'It is necessary to acknowledge and work through this pain or it will manifest itself through some symptoms or other form of aberrant behaviour' (Worden, 1991: 13).

He says that society may make this difficult, since those around us when we are grieving find it difficult to manage our pain and often make this known, by saying such things as 'you ought to be over this by now', or by attempting to distract us from our grief. For those who are dealing with the loss of their fertility this process is rendered more difficult, I believe, by the 'invisible' nature of the loss, and many couples are confronted by people who say such things as 'aren't you lucky, you don't have to use birth control', or 'you can have my kids any time, you will soon be glad you don't have any!'. All of this makes it very difficult for infertile people to feel that they have anything to grieve over and adds to their sense of isolation and pain.

Some people will not allow themselves to feel at all, and focus on the next treatment or the fact that they can now have the better car, house, holiday, instead. Worden says that, 'One of the aims of grief counselling is to help facilitate people through this difficult task so they don't carry the pain with them throughout their life' (Worden, 1991: 14). He quotes John Bowlby, 'Sooner or later, some of those who avoid all conscious grieving, break down – usually with some form of depression' (Bowlby, 1980: 158).

The unseen nature of people's infertility means that it is all the more easy for those around them to discount their pain and to try to point out all the positive sides to child-free living, at the time when the individual or couple needs to feel that they are allowed to cry, rage and feel the pain of this enormous blow to their sense of themselves, their hopes and their aspirations.

Task 3 To adjust to an environment in which the [deceased] is missing

An adjustment must be made to a world in which, for the infertile person, the desired child is missing. This has to do with the final realisation of the actuality of this loss. Worden says that

> Not only do the bereaved have to adjust to the loss of roles previously played [by the deceased], but [death] also confronts them with the challenge of adjusting to their own sense of self. Recent studies posit that for women who define their identity through relationships and caring for others, bereavement means not only the loss of a significant other but also the sense of a loss of self (Zaiger, 1985). (Worden, 1991: 15)

For those facing their infertile state, this statement seems particularly pertinent. The potential child or children had roles already in this person's life and in the life of this couple. In many ways individuals choose partners for long-term intimate relationships, not only for themselves, but for their potential as father or mother to an envisaged family in the future. This is not necessarily done explicitly, but I believe it is done none the less. Many people have expressed their sadness that their spouse or partner will after all not be the biological parent to any child they might have. This expression is shown in the following example:

> *Rose*: I remember thinking what a great dad he would be. He still will be of course, but it is so sad that it won't be *his* child. I feel cheated. I won't be able to look at our child and know that these features come from Tom. I *chose* Tom not only as a husband but to be the father of my children. It's hard to have to let that dream go.

The loss of this 'potentiality' can have a devastating impact on the couple's relationship. One partner may view the infertile one as having let them and their relationship down. They may feel enormous sadness and pain that the child whom they were jointly to conceive will not now be anything like their imaginings. When a couple discover that, for them, conception will require various medical, possibly highly intrusive, interventions, they are *already* in the position of having to face a loss. For most couples, conception is an intensely private event. Infertility treatments often result in the loss of privacy. Conception, should it occur, will be a public event. They have also lost the story of conception, which may be a part of the overall story of *their* family. They have lost the images that so far they will have had of themselves, as parents, as 'lucky', as 'in control'. They have lost direction in their lives.

This statement from a client seems to me to illustrate this sense of loss well.

> obviously, you're born, then you have your period, then you start going out with someone and you get married, and then have your children. Later, you have your menopause . . . we'd been quite careful, planning our money, doing the house, get that all done, and then children . . . .

For this couple, the abrupt onset of early menopause had put a halt to their plans and had confronted them with the loss of control over the direction of their lives, as well as, for the woman, the loss of an image of herself as a young woman.

Task 4   To emotionally relocate the [deceased] and move on with life

Worden states there is a need to be able to reinvest emotional energy in life, to feel creative and energised again.

> The counsellor's task [then] becomes not to help the bereaved give up their relationship with [the deceased] but to help them find an appropriate place for [the dead] in their emotional lives – a place that will enable them to go on living effectively in the world. (Worden, 1991: 17)

This is especially important for those at the end of fertility treatments, whose task is to learn to 're-invent' their lives without children, and to take pleasure and meaning from a world in which their own biological, and perhaps any, children are missing.

Egan: a helping model

The third model that I wish to introduce is that developed by Inskipp (1986) from the work of Gerard Egan, in his book *The*

Skilled Helper (1981), in which he developed a three-stage model of helping. This has been outlined in the following manner.

Stage 1 Exploration

The helper, by developing a warm relationship, enables the client to explore 'the problem' from their frame of reference, and then to focus on specific concerns. According to Inskipp (1986: 20) the *skills* which are used to facilitate this are:

- Attention giving.
- Listening.
- Active listening.
- Communicating empathetic understanding.
- Non-critical acceptance by paraphrasing, reflecting feelings, summarising.
- Helping the client to be specific.

For the counsellor in an infertility unit this first stage is crucially important in the establishment of sufficient rapport with the individual or couple to allow them to feel understood and confident enough to ask questions and to consider counselling helpful to them. This is the time when the counsellor will let the client(s) know that there may be difficult and painful feelings for them and that counselling is available to them throughout any treatment or investigations (if it is), should they wish it. They are most likely to consider counselling later if a good rapport has been established at this early point.

Stage 2 New understanding

Clients are helped to see themselves and their situation in new perspectives, and to focus on what they might do to cope more effectively. They are helped to see what strengths and resources they might use.

The following *skills* are needed here (Inskipp, 1986: 20):

- Communicating deeper empathic understanding using 'hunches'.
- Helping the client recognise themes and inconsistencies.
- Giving information.
- Sharing the helpers' feelings and/or experiences (self-disclosure).
- Immediacy. That is, you–me talk, what is happening between us now.
- Goal setting.

These are *challenging skills* and are used with the skills of the exploration stage. These may be used in addition to those outlined in Stage 1, and at any time during the counselling process.

However, when a couple is faced with particularly difficult feelings, such as anger or grief, these skills can be most effectively employed, thus moving them towards a position where they may feel more energetic and able to act.

Stage 3   Action
The client is helped to consider possible ways to act, to look at costs and consequences, to plan action, implement it and evaluate.

The *skills* involved here (Inskipp, 1986: 20) are those of both Stages 1 and 2 as well as:

- Creative thinking and brainstorming.
- Problem solving and decision making.
- The use of learning theory to plan action.
- Evaluation.

Choosing different courses of action, balancing options and acting in one's own and most appropriate best interest is the task of Stage 3. The skills of the counsellor in helping the client(s) to think creatively, solve problems and to plan and evaluate action are needed at this time.

This model seems to me a very helpful way of managing the counselling interaction, which is both focused and specific. For example, clients who are in the early stages of managing their infertility problem may initially need assurance that the pain and confusion that they may be experiencing are 'normal', and the skills needed may be those of Stage 1, namely, asking open-ended questions and communicating empathically through active listening and paraphrasing. On the other hand, those who are at the point of having their fifth IVF attempt may need recognition of the depression that they may be experiencing and skills in each of the stages may be used.

Infertility Counselling Model

I now want to introduce the fourth model that I mentioned at the beginning of this chapter. Through my work, in both public and private health care settings, where I have worked as the manager/counsellor of a DI unit, and as a counsellor for IVF and ovum donation programmes, I have developed a model which I have characterised as having five phases. Counselling may be beneficial at any one or all of these phases.

1 Diagnosis

When a fertility problem is diagnosed, clients may feel shocked and distressed, and respond by denying the diagnosis, or its importance, and withdrawing from others. This would roughly correspond with Kubler-Ross's first stage. The task here, as Worden would describe it, is to help the clients to acknowledge the reality of their situation, and I would see this as being done by using Egan's Stage 1 skills of active listening, reflection of feelings, summarising and focusing, to facilitate the exploration of this event with the clients.

2 Managing feelings

In this phase the feelings that the couple may be experiencing need to be acknowledged, worked with and placed in the context of their understanding of themselves, their roles in relation to each other and their families. What has been their view of themselves in their world? Are they people who are unused to not getting what they want? How does this event impact their sense of worth, their relationships, their sexuality, their sense of who they are? 'Couples told us of the challenges that infertility presented to their emotional balance, self esteem, and perspectives regarding the controllability and fairness of life' (Stanton and Dunkel-Schetter, 1991: xi). This phase is analogous to Kubler-Ross's Anger stage and Worden's task of working through the pain of grief. The counsellor may use the skills in Egan's Stage 1 as before, as well as those in Stage 2, particularly in communicating deeper empathic understanding.

3 Planning action

This is the phase where couples feel ready to move on, to start to make decisions and to take greater control over the direction of their lives in terms of their fertility, investigation and treatment. Bargaining, as described in Kubler-Ross's Stage 3, may be one of the ways in which they begin to do this, and there will be a need on the counsellor's part to take this couple through this stage and to continue to facilitate them in their adjustment to this crisis in their lives. Egan's Stage 2 skills of recognition of themes, giving information, immediacy and goal setting are especially relevant here. The skills outlined in the Action stage of the Egan model may also be suitably used here, that is the consideration of options, costs and consequences and evaluation.

4 Having treatment

When couples start to have treatment, they may find that they have many differing responses to it. There may be a sense of excitement that something is happening at last; there may be a fear of what the effects of the treatment may be on them or their spouse/partner, either physically or emotionally. There may also be a fear about whether this is going 'to work'. If there has been any lingering, secret hope that a pregnancy would happen 'normally', having treatment may confront this and cause the infertile person or couple to feel depressed and confused, at the very moment when they thought that they would feel most hope and anticipation. Thus, couples may question themselves, their motives, the clinic, the counsellor, in what may appear to be a last minute rush of panic.

The counsellor, when helping people at this point in the infertility treatment process, will perhaps need to make explicit what was an implicit denial of the reality of their infertility.

5 Awaiting outcomes

The time when couples are awaiting the results of tests or treatment procedures is often a very difficult one for both partners, since they are wanting to be both realistic about the chances of conception, and hopeful regarding conception. It is difficult for couples to know what to think, or how to feel, and many are unable to do more than 'close down' on their emotions. Others become very excited in anticipation of a pregnancy. Kubler-Ross's fifth stage and Worden's fourth task are achieved in so far as the decision to have treatment, and letting go of having their own biological child, in the case of gamete donation, or of having a child without third party intervention, can be seen as an acceptance of their loss and that they are emotionally relocating their energies into achieving parenthood in this way. The use of the skills of Egan's Stages 1, 2 and 3 will be needed here. Figure 2.1 shows the Infertility Counselling Model (ICM).

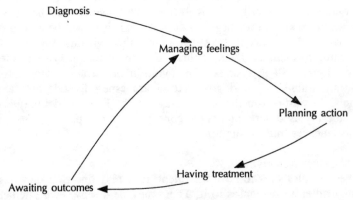

Figure 2.1 *The Infertility Counselling Model*

Kubler-Ross stages	Worden tasks	Egan stages	ICM phases
Denial and Isolation	Acknowledge reality of situation	Exploration	Diagnosis
Anger	Work through pain of grief		Managing feelings
Bargaining	Adjusting to environment without the person	New understanding	Planning action
Depression		Action	Having treatment
Acceptance	To emotionally relocate and move on		Awaiting outcomes

Figure 2.2 *An overview of the models for use in fertility counselling*

Kubler-Ross's stages and Worden's tasks describe the *processes* that people need to go through in order to resolve healthily their grief about their losses. Egan's stages show the *skills* which the counsellor uses to assist clients through these processes. The Infertility Counselling Model (ICM) describes the journey of the infertile person or couple through their infertility and its treatment and management. This process is underpinned and informed by the stages and tasks of Kubler-Ross and Worden. Egan's skills are used to facilitate the individual or couple through this process. Figure 2.2 shows how the different models interconnect.

For example, when a person has had a diagnosis of infertility (ICM), they may move into Denial and Isolation (Kubler-Ross, Stage 1) as discussed earlier in this chapter. An exploration (Egan, Stage 1) of this will be with the goal of helping the person to acknowledge the reality of their situation (Worden, Task 1). From this the management of the feelings about their situation (ICM) is analogous to Stage 2 of Kubler-Ross, the Anger phase, and Task 2 of Worden, working through the pain of the grief. The skills here will be Egan's Stage 1 skills also. This can be generally followed throughout the diagram as indicated. However, unless couples are ending treatment permanently, when the last stages and tasks are clearly relevant, the individual or couple will go through the process again after Awaiting Outcomes, starting with the Managing Feelings stage and moving down again.

It is apparent that there is a cyclical quality to the work with infertile people, who may go through a 'shortened' form of the total grieving process that Kubler-Ross and Worden have described. For example, each time a treatment intervention does not have the desired outcome of pregnancy, couples may experience a 'mini' grief process, which I see essentially as a minor expression of a greater underlying grief and existential anxiety. They may not allow themselves to feel this at this time, since if they did, they may feel unable to make decisions about their next step in treatment. This way of managing the infertility experience is often subtly and probably unconsciously endorsed by clinics. Clinic staff wish to have as many 'successes' as possible and may continue to offer further medical interventions as quickly as they can, under considerable pressure from the clients (who often feel greatly pressured by time). Staff respond as they have been trained to do, with a prescription to 'make it better'. It may well only be when treatment finally ends that couples feel able to experience a complete expression of the mourning process. This is often at the time when the clinic discharges them and they are left to their own devices, not only managing the end of their hope for a child, but the loss of a whole network and structure in their lives, which has been an intense part of their lives, often for many years.

I visualise the above process in the way shown in Figure 2.3. Thus, the 'Feelings' stage is omitted in the desire and the hurry to solve the problem as quickly as possible.

From the point of diagnosis of a fertility problem, where many couples may, as previously noted, respond by withdrawal from potential support networks and with a need to take action as a way of gaining control in a situation that essentially feels out of hand, couples may experience strong emotions, and either work through these appropriately or go straight into treatment programmes.

The point of diagnosis is where I think it is important that those in the clinic setting need to be alert to the possibility that couples or individuals may need to be allowed time to work through their feelings with a counsellor or other trained professional, so that decisions about treatment may be made effectively. In a text in which many different contributors have been brought together to consider the subject of infertility from the viewpoint of stress and stress reactions, one of the editors states:

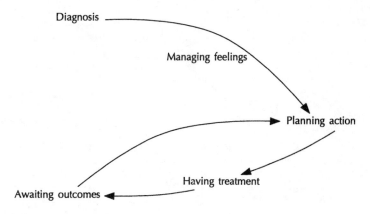

Figure 2.3 *The ICM showing the exclusion of 'managing feelings' stage*

The psychological literature reveals consistently that appraising a threatening encounter as unchangeable or uncontrollable impedes adjustment (Folkman et al., 1986a; Taylor et al., 1984). In infertility, the couple experiences a loss of control in an arena typically assumed to be controllable (i.e. the ability to bear children). Many writers (e.g. Cook, 1987; Mahlstedt, 1985) suggest that distress is a likely result. Thus, conclusions the infertile individual reaches during the appraisal process would be expected to contribute to his or her psychological adjustment. (Stanton, 1991: 89)

The counsellor is in a position to help at this crucial phase of the couple's infertility process and needs to be aware of the person's reactions to their diagnosis and help them to gain a level of expression, understanding and control in this situation. 'Those who appraise infertility as carrying a high potential for harm or little potential for benefit might be particularly likely to experience distress' (Stanton, 1991: 89).

The cycle of planning action–having treatment–awaiting results–planning action, and so on, is one with which many working with couples in infertility units will be familiar. Looked at in the medical context, this makes good sense, and is usually what the patients want. In the context of the significance and meaning of a diagnosis of infertility, it would seem important to slow this process down, to take account of the need to allow the expression of feeling and the placing of this event in the couple's joint and individual lives. So, the process would be as shown in Figure 2.4.

This whole process is complicated by the infertile couple's

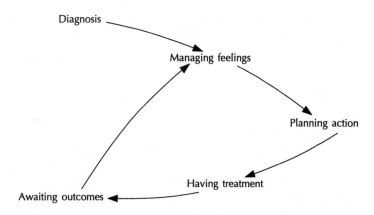

Figure 2.4 *The ICM showing the inclusion of the 'managing feelings' stage*

demands to have the medical profession come up with an answer, and preferably a pregnancy, very quickly. Medical professionals are trained to respond to this demand. I make the point that this is not always in the best interests of the patients'/clients' long-term adjustment, either to infertility, or to having children through any of the medical interventions or techniques. In the following chapters I will concentrate on the issues raised when working with the initial diagnosis of a fertility problem, the management of the adjustment to infertility, and the planning and reinvestment phases.

3

Facing the Key Issues

The issues that face those with a fertility problem may include *fear* that they are '*abnormal*'. Many experience a loss of *self esteem* as well as a sense that they are not in *control* of the direction of their lives. They may face an *existential anxiety*, asking themselves questions regarding the *purpose* of their lives. These questions are 'What am I here for?', and 'How do I define myself in the world?' There may be fears about how they can take their place in their world, and fears about a life that stretches ahead of them with no children to occupy their time and energy. They may ask themselves, 'What do I do with my life if there are no children?'

People who receive a diagnosis of infertility typically respond with shock and denial (Kubler-Ross, Stage 1; Worden, Task 1). This reaction has been described as a 'life crisis', with its resultant feelings of loss of self esteem, fear and panic. 'Suddenly a young healthy adult has a medical label – a devastating stigma – thrust upon them. The one "at fault" feels neutered, unattractive – a "freak of nature"' (Mostyn, 1992: 32). Mostyn says that for most a diagnosis of infertility is completely unexpected.

This chapter will explore how people present these fears in the counselling interview and how the counsellor may work with them so that the infertile person or couple may make decisions and choices and begin to re-assume control. When an individual or a couple is confronted with a fertility problem any of the issues of fear, abnormality, loss of self esteem, loss of control or existential anxiety may become the focus of distress. For some the sense of being out of control of their lives is terrifying and unfamiliar and may lead to feelings of panic. Some may experience panic attacks or outbursts of painful weeping, as was the case with Zoe (see Chapter 2). Others may respond by attempting to exert as much control over the situation as they can. This may be seen when someone seems to become over-controlling about treatments or appointment times, or within relationships. Still others may be less concerned about having a child and more about finding out what is wrong with them.

Shapiro makes the point that 'Some couples search more for an answer than a pregnancy' (1988: 130).

There are several ways in which an individual or couple may come to realise that they have a fertility problem. When a person is diagnosed as infertile, the diagnosis may come as a shock. They will often react with disbelief, asking that tests be repeated, demanding to see somebody else, asking whether this could be a mistake. The task of giving 'bad news' is often the nurse's or doctor's. Many medical staff are used to giving such information, but may need help and support to manage it more effectively. At such times access to a counsellor may be useful, as a resource for the medical team as well as for the client. Having a counsellor available and accessible to whom clients may be referred after such news has been given is now a necessary and appropriate part of the provision of a complete infertility clinic service. Thus counsellors may be presented with couples or individuals who have heard such devastating news very recently. The counsellor will need to use Egan's Stage 1 skills of giving attention and of active listening (see Chapter 2, p. 31). They will also need to be able to give appropriate explanations about what this information means and what the possible next steps may be. As in any crisis counselling, the counsellor needs to appear calm and in control, and be able and prepared to guide the couple or individual through this early period of adjustment. Clinical experience suggests that clients are reassured where the counsellor is not overwhelmed by the clients' feelings and experience.

The first appointment will be one in which the infertile person or couple is provided with the framework for the next step in the process. This might be, for example, gaining further information from another source, talking to partners, friends and family or taking some reading material away to look at. The infertile person or couple will retain only certain amounts of information at this time. Assessing their ability to take in and understand new information is an important part of the counsellor's role. They will need to be assured of the availability of the counsellor, within the appropriate time constraints, and that the couple or individual can contact them or other members of staff for information when they feel ready to do so. The sensitive and careful management of this first shock may have an enormous impact on how the individual or couple experience and adjust to their infertility.

In other cases, however, the diagnosis of an infertility problem may confirm a suspicion that has been growing, and may initially be experienced as a relief. For some, the awareness that there is or will be a problem in conceiving has grown slowly over a considerable time, and thus when this is confirmed there is a sense of relief that something definite has been found to explain what has been happening. In most cases it is the possibility rather than the reality of infertility that is at issue, because there is some degree of ambiguity about the outcome. This has been described in the following way: 'This situation initially involves a threat rather than a loss (Lazarus, 1966; Lazarus and Launier, 1978; Lazarus and Folkman, 1984). As time passes without conception, the situation is gradually transformed into one of loss' (Dunkel-Schetter and Lobel, 1991: 29).

It is at this point, when the infertile person seeks help, possibly under pressure from a spouse or partner, that there may be a sense of relief at the acknowledgement of the fertility problem. It is possible that for a proportion of this group there has been an element of denial (Kubler-Ross, Stage 1). They may also have isolated themselves from support, perhaps due to feelings of shame.

For others, infertility may be the result of medical or surgical intervention, and thus the couple or individual has known that this was likely to be the case. Infertility may for example, be the 'side effect' of treatment for cancer or another life threatening condition. It is possible in these cases to see infertility as the 'lesser evil'. As such, infertility may be grieved as one of many losses, and the task of the counsellor is to help the person or couple manage and deal with their feelings, in the way and in the order which they themselves prioritise.

Alternatively, the person or couple may feel that they wish to move on to deciding on a treatment programme quickly. The counsellor needs to assess whether this is an aspect of denial, or whether in this case the couple or individual has had sufficient time and support to have worked through the issues that their infertility raises for them. There are some questions that the counsellor may ask at this stage to elicit this understanding.

Useful questions for the counsellor

- How long have you known that there is a fertility problem?
- How did you react/feel when you first understood that there was a fertility problem?
- How has this affected you? (as individuals)
- How has this affected your relationship, including your sexual relationship?
- Who else knows that you have a fertility problem?
- What has been their reaction to this?
- Have you had any other help or counselling about this? If yes, what helped and what hindered?

The answers to these questions help the counsellor to understand what the couple's or individual's needs are now, and whether it is appropriate to move on with making decisions about treatment. If the couple or individual exhibit signs of confusion, isolation or panic, this would indicate a need to allow them more time before deciding on the next stage of investigation or treatment. This time would be used to help the individual or couple to understand what their infertility means *for them*, encouraging them to find support amongst family or friends, or in extra counselling, and in exploring what has been the impact of their infertility on them as individuals and on the couple relationship.

Case example

Janet and Robert had been referred for ovum donation shortly after Janet was diagnosed as having gone through a premature menopause at the age of 26. In the first part of the interview the counsellor's task is to clarify what their infertility has meant for them and for their relationship. The counselling then develops, the couple begin to share with the counsellor and with each other their deeper fears that this life event has raised for them. The key issues that arise for this couple are fear and loss of control.

Counsellor: I understand that the problem is that you have gone through a premature menopause?
Janet: Yes.
Counsellor: That must be devastating for you both.

The counsellor clearly indicates here that the premature menopause that Janet has undergone is seen as a joint problem for the couple. They may have different responses to this but it is a fertility problem for *them*.

Janet: Yes.
Counsellor: Yes, it sounds as though it shocked you.
Robert: I was shattered.
Counsellor: Shattered . . .
Robert: I've sort of come to terms with it now.
Janet: We found out in June.
Robert: That's one summer I won't forget. Since then things have got better, and I feel a lot more hopeful.
Janet: When my friend phoned and said that she wanted to donate her eggs, that was really nice, really emotional. I know that she will be the best donor.

Here, Janet appears to be wanting to move straight ahead with planning treatment. The counsellor brings them back to exploring what effect their infertility has had on them. This is done with the aim of ensuring that the couple, and in particular Janet, are not attempting to avoid her feelings about what has happened and move quickly from Stage 1 to Stage 3 (Egan). That is, from the Exploration to the Action stage.

> *Counsellor*: How has this news affected the two of you? This is still recent information for you.
>
> *Janet*: It makes you more aware of what happens in life. You just take it for granted that you are going to get married, have a baby, but it's not as easy as that.
>
> *Robert*: I think initially I just couldn't believe it. It was just such a shock, it knocked me for six. It affected my work as well, I thought about it constantly.

Here, Robert is describing a response that is common for many. The difficulty in concentrating at work, the continual pondering about the situation, the sense of disbelief, are all 'normal' experiences. Many infertile people find that for a time they are constantly thinking about their situation, and that this affects their ability to function as effectively as previously in the workplace. This is often at the time when those around them are suggesting that they immerse themselves in work, or to try to 'forget about it' (the infertility). Because this is almost impossible to do, people often feel even less in control, that they are 'going crazy', and feel even less confident at work. The job of the counsellor in this case is to assure the person, by giving the relevant information, that their response is a 'normal' response to a shocking event and that it will pass.

This couple had had some support from their families but were feeling quite low, although during this interview Janet exhibited a range of feelings from excitement that something might be done to help them achieve a pregnancy, to sadness that this had happened to her. The counsellor continues to clarify events and to ascertain what is going on for this couple now.

> *Counsellor*: What is it that seems to be the most difficult part for you now?
>
> *Janet*: I wonder why it hasn't worked out the way we wanted it to. We'd been careful, planning our money, getting the house done, doing it all properly.
>
> *Robert*: It's been like a kick in the teeth.

Counsellor: So you've been wondering what you have done to deserve this?
Robert: Yes, that's it.
Counsellor: And this has been a shock to your sense of your progress through your lives, where you were going, and what you were doing, is that right?
Janet: Yes, I've felt a bit at a loss really. I've been really excited about coming here today. It feels like I'm doing something.

In this example it is possible to see that the couple's belief system has been confronted by the diagnosis of Janet's infertility. This system appears to operate on the premise that: 'If we behave properly, and do the right things, then we deserve to have our lives the way we want them.' There seems to be an implicit assumption that there is a reason behind life events, and a consequent difficulty in managing the apparent randomness of what has happened to them. This idea is fairly usual and brings with it the resultant sense of guilt and blame that logically follows such a belief. This is an example of the *existential need for certainty* and thus one of the *key issues* discussed at the beginning of this chapter. It may also be an expression of Kubler-Ross's Bargaining stage described in Chapter 2.

The key issues for this couple have begun to emerge in the above example. Concerns about *abnormality* as well as *fear* of the future, and a loss of *self esteem* are clearly what Janet is struggling with. Robert is more concerned with *control* issues and it is noteworthy that Robert states most clearly his sense of shock at the diagnosis that Janet was now infertile. For him this may reflect a feeling of panic that his life plan has now been threatened by circumstances that are beyond his control. For Janet there is a sense of bewilderment, and a tendency to discount her pain and confusion. She seemed to need to feel that there were possible solutions to her infertility as well as a need to understand what had caused her premature menopause. It may be that her desire to push forward with treatment options was an expression of denying the significance of this diagnosis. Looking at this in terms of the model presented in the previous chapter, it may be that Janet is denying her feelings, as shown in Figure 3.1. Robert seems to have acknowledged his initial feelings of shock and panic to a greater extent, as described in Figure 3.2.

The counsellor has to make a judgement, sometimes on the basis of one counselling interview, about where each individual is within the model. Having made such an assessment, the question 'what needs to be done next?' arises. Again, some questions may clarify this.

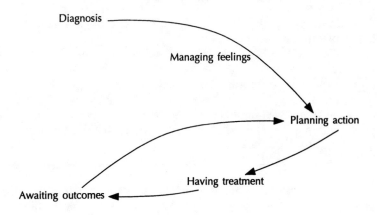

Figure 3.1   *The ICM showing Janet's denial of feelings*

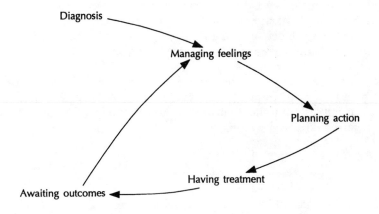

Figure 3.2   *The ICM showing Robert's acknowledgement of feelings*

Useful questions for the counsellor

- Is it appropriate for this couple to move on to treatment planning?
- Do they, as a couple, or individually, need further counselling?
- What would be the goal of such counselling?
- Does the counsellor have a sense that there is sufficient awareness, support, communication and understanding within this couple, that *on balance* no further pre-treatment counselling need be done?

Answers to these questions will enable the counsellor to clarify the progress of the couple, to plan what may be the next stage in counselling, and to evaluate what has been done so far.

The task of the counsellor is often to model for the couple the skill of *staying with* the anxiety. This is important so that the couple learn that they can survive the painful feelings that arise, and allows them to make effective and autonomous choices, rather than rushing into *any* action to avoid such discomfort. On page 42 above we saw how Janet seemed to want to move straight ahead with treatment, and the counsellor returned them to how they had been feeling about their infertility.

In the next example, the key issues are loss of self esteem, fear about not being 'normal', and loss of control. The couple are facing a difficult task in trying to determine how they might live together if there should be no children.

Case example

Nada and Ahmed had been referred for counselling before deciding whether to have ovum donation. They had had several IVF attempts that had not been successful. Nada had been shocked and distressed when she realised that her fallopian tubes had been so badly damaged by a burst appendix when she was a teenager that she would be unable to conceive 'naturally'.

Counsellor: You noticed that you weren't getting pregnant, and you went to the doctor.
Nada: Yes, I thought I would just check, just in case.
Counsellor: And what happened then?
Nada: They did two laparoscopies.
Counsellor: What effect did that have on you?

Nada: It was a bit of a shock. When I had the first laparoscopy, I could hear what was going on in the theatre, that's what made it worse. I was in the recovery room and I could hear what they were saying. You know, wait until she hears the story. And I thought 'Oh no,' I knew then. That was a shock and I just wanted to find out what it was. They wouldn't tell you exactly when you woke up, so that was why I was shocked to hear it.

Counsellor: Yes.

Ahmed: It did feel more relaxed when we went up to the hospital. We realised that we are not the only ones, you know. There were so many persons, different people more badly off than us.

Counsellor: So you then realised that it was going to be, well difficult if not impossible to conceive in the usual way?

The counsellor here is exploring and clarifying the situation with the couple, and getting an understanding of the couple's journey thus far, as well as the impact that their experiences may have had upon them. The counsellor is using Egan's Stage 1 skills of focusing and asking open-ended questions to facilitate the couple's expression of their situation and their feelings about their infertility.

The counsellor is not attempting to work with the issues as such. The couple, with the help of the counsellor, go on to explain, for the first time, their shock at the diagnosis.

Nada: I couldn't believe it, I always expected, you know because my family are originally Turkish and they have so many children, I thought I was going to be the same, and I just couldn't believe it. It was a burst appendix that did the damage. My appendix burst when I was quite young.

Counsellor: How has this affected both of you, this difficulty in having children?

Note here that Nada expresses her disbelief at what had happened, and that this is her expression of denial, consistent with Kubler-Ross's first stage and Worden's first task. It became clear that Nada was devastated by her infertility and that her *self esteem* had been badly hurt by this diagnosis. Despite having had infertility treatments over some months, this woman still had a need to go through the story of the discovery of her infertility. The counsellor's role here was to facilitate this by asking questions, listening and responding empathically. The exploration of the story in this way (Egan, Stage 1) serves to allow Nada to feel that her experience is important and valid. She talked, laughingly and self deprecatingly, of her husband finding someone else who would be able to give him a family.

Counsellor: You've been through a lot of disappointments, and that's hard and very stressful, so the question I'm going to ask isn't easy, which is how are you going to feel if after several attempts, you don't conceive?

Ahmed: Is it possible that that should happen?
Counsellor: It is not certain that it will work.

The counsellor is facing Ahmed with the reality of the fact that fertility treatment does not always result in a pregnancy.

Nada: No, it wouldn't be the end of the world. You know, I've said to my husband, if he wants to find somebody else, then he can.
Ahmed: What else could we do if it doesn't work?

Here the couple are on two different tacks. The counsellor must decide which to follow. The counsellor chooses to stay with the issues raised by Nada, since it seems important to clarify what difficulties their relationship has, and how much Nada's self esteem is bound up with having a child.

Nada: I think I've done what I can, that's it.
Counsellor: Is that a decision that you have come to now?
Nada: Just maybe it's not meant to be, if it doesn't work, that's it.
Counsellor: How does it feel for you if you were never able to have a child?
Nada: Well, because I've done IVF first you tend to forget about it, once you've been away from it, so I said to myself it's not the end of the world and I think that's the way I would look at it again. It's just that when you keep doing it, that's when it's always on your mind, but when you don't do it, you've forgotten about it.
Ahmed: But one thing, hope never dies, you always think you are going to have one. You really are. I mean I don't know why exactly, at least in myself I always think we are going to have one, yes, just a question of time maybe.
Counsellor: It's seems important for you, Ahmed, especially, to have children. Would it be difficult for you never to have children?

The counsellor here returns to the issues raised by Ahmed earlier in the session.

Ahmed: I consider it very important for marriage, creating a family, I don't know maybe I am a little old fashioned or whatever you call it.
Counsellor: It sounds like that's how you understood your life was going to be.
Ahmed: I have a big family, you see. It is like being cut out from the others somehow. All my brothers, they have children, I am the only one left. I'm left out.
Counsellor: This has been very hard for you to see your brothers with their children?
Ahmed: Yes. Very hard.
Counsellor: So it is very important for you and it is clearly important for both of you in terms of how you see your life together.
Ahmed: Yes.
Counsellor: I've heard you say, Nada, that if it doesn't work Ahmed can find somebody else.

Nada: It's just the way I am, I don't like him to be without children, I mean in that way. I'd hate for him to stay with me and not have any children, because I've seen him, he just loves children. [*Here Nada begins to cry.*]

Counsellor: It sounds like it is very painful for you to feel that way. I know this is hard. Can you say a little about what makes you feel sad right now.

Nada: I'm just saying it's obviously hard that he would go off, you see, I don't want that to happen.

Counsellor: Is that something that is almost agreed between you, that if there aren't children you will separate?

Ahmed: No you are wrong. It seems that she only wants this if I want this. I would like for her to want to have this child even if I didn't exist.

Counsellor: Is that accurate for you? Are you doing this for him to have a child?

Nada: No, it's just that I've been through so much that I've just had enough of it really, it's just not easy to keep having all those injections, there were so many. I've just had enough.

Counsellor: It's seems that this has been an enormously stressful time for both of you.

Ahmed: Yes.

Ahmed was not feeling the same sorts of feelings as Nada, and was more focused on the goal of achieving a pregnancy. His main concern seemed to be that his wife was not at this point driven to pursue this goal with the same energy. She seemed to be both sad and angry and apparently a little resistant to doing *anything at all* to achieve a pregnancy. For the counsellor this difference between the individuals within a couple, where they are in their own process of the management of their joint infertility, can create a tension. The individuals within this particular couple seem to be at different points in their response to their infertility. Ahmed is at the point of discussing his need for the appearance of normality, whereas Nada is describing her shock and is feeling different and excluded. She also appears to be needing to grieve the loss of her fertility while he is wanting to move ahead with getting a family. The counsellor *could* choose here to reflect the difference in their positions in the following way:

Counsellor: It seems that you both have different needs at the moment. Ahmed, you seem to want to have a clear idea of what to do next, and you seem very focused on getting access to any treatment that might work. You are also saying that you wish that Nada was doing this too. Perhaps this indicates that you feel isolated, and unsure of what to do, perhaps out of control. Nada, you are clearly distressed about what has happened, and I wonder if what you are wanting is for Ahmed to show you that he understands that. Perhaps while he is busy moving on with getting treatments, you are wanting him to slow down and take more account of your needs. Perhaps one of the things we could do is to work together to help you both feel more understood by the other?

This problem of the individuals in a couple being at different stages in their process, and how the counsellor might manage the tension that this creates, will be discussed further in Chapter 8.

The couple in this case also have different agendas in the counselling process, and it is important for the counsellor to clarify this with them in the way described. Nada has felt so undermined by the failure of the IVF treatments she has gone through that she feels ambivalent about embarking on further treatments. Her self esteem, already badly hurt by the original diagnosis, has been further battered by the subsequent attempts to conceive. For Ahmed, his sense of his place within his family of origin is under threat, and his need to have a child or children is so closely linked with his sense of purpose in his life, that he is highly motivated to continue treatments and reluctant to consider the possibility of 'failure'. Ahmed's need for Nada to feel the same way as he does about having children may indicate a need to feel that he is not isolated. Her need is for strength and self confidence, and she was clearly finding it difficult to feel valued unless she was able to conceive, and feeling resentful that ovum donation was the only possibility left to her. To some extent they are both struggling with the need to adhere to culturally prescribed roles.

The meanings of fertility, of conception, pregnancy, birth and childrearing are all relevant here, in that there will be differing emphases, and it is important that these are made overt and are understood between the couple or individual and the counsellor, since these are the areas of loss that will be most painfully felt, and may be most carefully defended. For Ahmed, there is a need to be a father, to fit into his family, to do what men in his family do, which includes having a child which is biologically his. If any further treatments are unsuccessful, it would then be the time to work with Ahmed on his grief for that loss. At this point he is still defending against this possibility. For Nada, her sense of herself as a wife and as a woman is threatened, her self esteem is low, she clearly feels to blame, and is trying to absolve herself of this by suggesting that he find someone else, although this is not what she wants. Nada would be willing to try for adoption, and it seems more important for her to have a role as a mother than to have a biological link to a child. This may be an indication that she is coming to accept that she is infertile and will need to rely on someone else's genetic material, if she is to have a birth child.

An analogy with the situation of a person facing a bereavement seems to be a useful one when looking at what has occurred for both the couples discussed in this chapter. For both there was a sense of shock and disbelief at the discovery of their infertility. They are then thrust into painful and distressing feelings and this is followed by the need to be proactive in some way, to take charge of the situation. When someone dies there is, depending on the nature of the death, shock and a sense of unreality. There are, however, things to do, telling people what has happened, arranging the funeral and so on. These are all necessary, and allow the person to feel initially that they have some control over what has happened. The feelings of pain and distress, the impact of what has happened and all that it means come later, perhaps over many weeks and months. The difference when a couple is diagnosed as having a fertility problem, is that it is not, in itself, usually a clearly defined event. Efforts to exert control over it are thus often frustrating and disempowering rather than serving a useful function.

> Perceptions of personal control figure prominently in most accounts of how people adapt to threatening events (Klinger, 1975; Kobasa, 1979; Langer and Rodin, 1976; Miller, 1980; Seligman, 1975; Suls and Mullen, 1981). There is now abundant evidence that individuals facing acute or modifiable stressors are well served by the belief that they can control outcomes. But for a prolonged crisis like impaired fertility, personal control beliefs may be ineffective and even counterproductive. By trying to produce the desired outcome, an individual may miss the *opportunity* to accommodate to this threatening situation and prepare for alternative outcomes. (Tennen et al., 1991: 110; emphasis added)

Couples may not see that there is a need to take the 'opportunity' to accommodate to this new situation, in their rush to 'fix it'. The medical profession may see it as their job to 'fix it' and so will not necessarily allow the time needed for the couple to adjust. It is the role of the counsellor to help the couple to take that time and in doing so the couple may feel paradoxically more in control of their choices. This is an important aim for counsellors in their work with the infertile person or couple since the evidence suggests that those who do manage this process in this way do better in terms of their adjustment to their infertility: 'Both females and males who felt greater control over the course of their fertility problem evidenced higher well-being, and the women also reported less distress' (Stanton, 1991: 97).

The following example shows how the *key issues* of *control, fear* and *existential anxiety* may manifest themselves in a very powerful way.

Case example

Charlotte, a woman aged 41 years, was referred during her last cycle of treatment that would end in an embryo transfer (ET). She had not sought counselling but had been given implications counselling (see Chapter 1) by the clinic as part of the procedures she went through to obtain IVF, something that she had found irrelevant and unhelpful. She was a highly successful professional woman who had been married for 10 years and who ran a business with her husband. She presented in a very agitated state, laughing, fidgeting and crying in turn. She was very clear, however, that part of what was so distressing was that she felt so out of control of events. She said that she had known that her husband might have a fertility problem when they got married, but had said to herself that it would not be a problem, and that they could sort it out between them. She had never considered the possibility of 'failure'. She clearly felt that *she* was a failure for not being able to *make it* happen. As she said:

> I never thought that I couldn't do it. As long as I worked hard for it as I have for everything else, I could have what I wanted. I always thought that of course I was fertile and that I would have a baby. I don't know what to do. I am absolutely terrified of the future.

Charlotte was very angry, scared and desperate for something to *do*, so that she could feel in control of her fate. She was someone who had never been given, or taken, the chance to face the fears that her inability to have a child aroused in her; loss of control, fear of getting old, anger with 'god', and the fear that she would be permanently a child of her parents, not a parent herself. In the Infertility Counselling Model presented in Chapter 2, she had gone from diagnosis directly to planning action and having treatments, as described in Figure 3.3. Now, 4 years, later she was having to confront her fear.

Tennen et al. (1991), in choosing the word 'opportunity' in the passage we looked at above, have highlighted an important way of viewing this event, and one which Leick and Davidsen-Nielsen (1991) discuss in their work on *Healing Pain. Attachment, Loss and Grief Therapy*. There is a chance for people to use this experience in a way that allows them to feel stronger, and less afraid.

> A person's need to feel control, coherence and meaning in his life is great. From our earliest childhood we have been learning to master our life, learning to overcome chaos. Traumatic events mobilize our fear that the chaos will devour us. The emotions of grief are experienced by giving up control, giving way, abandoning ourselves to the feeling of

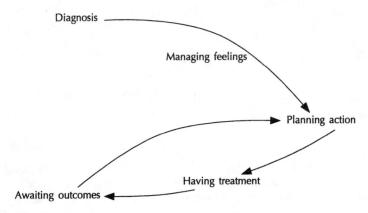

Figure 3.3 *The ICM showing Charlotte's avoidance of feelings*

chaos. The encounter with chaos and the uncontrollable aspect of existence paradoxically gives us strength and courage to live. (Leick and Davidsen-Nielsen, 1991: 22)

For Charlotte, while seeking counselling may have been partly a need to feel that she was doing *something*, it was a first step to managing the feelings that she was experiencing.

In all the examples in this chapter, control issues were beginning to surface, as well as the clients' existential fears about their place in the world and their role in life. Working with these in greater depth, and with feelings of loss, will be explored further in the following chapter.

4

Facing the Loss

This chapter discusses the issue of facing losses in infertility and is divided into two main areas. The first section explores a framework for managing the treatment process and will include brief examples and discussion. The second section continues the case history of Zoe, introduced in Chapter 2, who now needs to go through a recognition of her loss before she can move forward.

It is during the treatment phase that couples confront the reality of their loss. Each couple may experience a complex mixture of issues that are raised for them by this. The couple will also be likely to go through cycles of excitement, disappointment, distress and frustration, and may need intervention from the counsellor at different points of these cycles.

Anthony Reading makes an important point when he observes,

> As with other chronic conditions, the emphasis is on enhancing effective coping and reducing the toll taken by the problem so that the affected individual can achieve a satisfying life. The changing face of medical practice is setting new psychological challenges. Technology that offers hope also confers protracted uncertainty for many couples. (1991: 194)

This emphasis on effective coping is at the core of the management of the infertile couple as they progress through treatment stages. There seems to be a 'roller-coaster' effect, with the infertile couple swinging from hope to despair, from pain to joy, which the counsellor needs to help to modify. Modification of this effect has the aim of reducing the stress that the couple suffer. While the people involved in having treatments will respond in their own unique ways to the stresses that treatment puts on them, it is useful to have a general formulation for this process. What I want to do now is to set out a range of goals and pertinent questions for the counsellor to have in mind when working with the infertile person or couple during the different stages of the treatment processes, which are outlined in Figure 4.1.

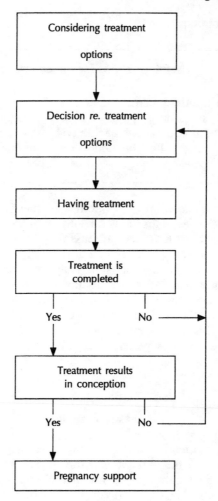

Figure 4.1 *Flow chart of the framework for working with the couple or individual during infertility treatment*

Treatment options

Useful questions for the counsellor

- What are the treatment options?
- What issues do they raise for the couple/individual?
- Are these options compatible with their value system?
- What might be the long-term consequences of any decision taken now?

What is acceptable for one infertile couple is unacceptable for another. What is important for one is irrelevant for another. Treatments, which in a medical sense may be the 'best' option, for some will be unacceptable, at least at this stage. They may choose a course of treatment that has apparently less chance of pregnancy, or which requires more organisation or inconvenience for the couple and possibly for the clinic. This needs to be understood as an attempt by the infertile couple to control what happens to them, and to 'fit' this new experience within the framework of their own value system. This is perhaps best illustrated with the following example.

Case example

Joe and Rose attended for counselling, regarding DI. They brought Joe's brother to the appointment too, since they were wanting to have 'known' donation using his sperm, as a way of overcoming their infertility. This required considerable organisation and inconvenience for them as well as for the clinic. Joe and Rose would have had treatment more quickly had they chosen to enter a DI programme and accepted anonymous donation. For them, however, three main factors were significant. First, both felt a strong need to know where the sperm had come from. Secondly, for Joe, in particular, the genetic link through his brother and thus to any child, was very important. Thirdly, they both felt that using anonymous sperm was almost as though Rose would be invaded sexually by possibly several donors. They did not feel this way about the use of his brother's sperm. This allowed both Joe and Rose to feel greater comfort and control over who was going to be 'inside' her vagina; control over the kind of person who would be the biological father of their child, and comfort coming from the 'fit' they had made with their value system.

Decision

Useful questions for the counsellor

- Have the couple or individual got enough information to feel that they can make a positive decision?
- Having made their decision, what do the couple or individual need to help them manage their feelings about this?

Most infertile people want to have a lot of information about the treatment so that they feel aware and in control of the process. Many want to have statistics about pregnancy and 'take home baby' rates. This is appropriate and the counsellor's role is to place the figures in context for the couple and relate them to their particular circumstances. It is sometimes difficult for the counsellor to avoid colluding with unrealistic expectations of 'success' that the couple may have and which may be part of the couple's denial of the reality of the situation. It is important to be realistic about the chances of conception and pregnancy.

Case example

A 43-year-old woman called Erica attended counselling during what was to be her last IVF attempt, having had four previous IVF treatments. During discussion the counsellor made the following statement, 'The reality is that the majority of those who have infertility treatment do not become pregnant as a result.' When Erica returned to the next session she said that no one had ever been that 'up-front' with her about the chances before. She felt angry because the counsellor was saying something that she did not want to hear. Erica also felt relief that most women do not conceive and thus that she was *not such a failure*. Her relief may also have been as a result of the understanding that the counsellor was prepared to confront her. This helped Erica to begin the process of grieving for the children she had not had and to feel the anger she was experiencing in a situation in which she had felt out of control.

In this case, Erica was stating very clearly that she just wanted a 'proper chance' to conceive, and that she was sure that she could. This can be seen as part of the Bargaining stage that Kubler-Ross describes (see Chapter 2). Shapiro has this to say about this phase of the work with infertile people.

> The helping professional must recognise bargaining behaviour as an effort to hold at bay the feelings of grief associated with infertility. An important function at this point is to help the infertile person with reality testing. One can communicate an understanding of the infertile person's wish to exhaust every possibility before 'giving up', while at the same time encouraging the person to acknowledge the statistical success associated with alternative treatments or the more advanced technologies. Infertile people may need to use this time to speak of the importance of doing all they can to explore even the most remote possibilities of successful treatment. Ultimately, they may be receptive to discussing the way in which their bargaining behaviour is proving frustrating, expensive, and anger producing, as chances of conception diminish. The sadness as each month passes without a pregnancy provides an opportunity for the professional to encourage active grieving for the birth child that seems increasingly elusive. (1988: 51)

Having treatment

Useful questions for the counsellor if treatment is not completed

- What are their feelings about this?
- What have they learned about the medical process that may help to inform further decisions?
- What have they learned about themselves that may affect their future choices?

Treatment may consist of a variety of drug regimes, scans, blood tests, surgical interventions, including egg collection, IVF or GIFT. Occasionally, a proposed course of treatment is not completed, for a variety of reasons. This is often called an 'abandoned' cycle. Often the couple feel that they have 'failed', that they have not been 'good enough', even that they have let the clinic staff down! There may a sense of despair and of hopelessness. Couples wonder if they will ever have the opportunity to see if they can get through a treatment, and have even a hope of pregnancy. This may be defined also as part of the Kubler-Ross Bargaining stage mentioned in

Chapter 2. They may feel frustrated and angry at the delay and expense that this has now caused. Again, the couple may deny any feelings about it and want to move swiftly ahead to planning the next step. The counsellor needs to create the environment for the infertile couple to manage and deal with their feelings, with the goal of enabling them to take control over their own treatment direction, as far as is possible.

> Ideally staff should have access to a mental health professional so that they can receive guidance and develop skills to prevent and deal with crises. Staff may become invested in positive outcomes and so may share the emotional ups and downs of patients, making it difficult to give dispassionate advice. This may become a problem when couples feel they have let staff down by failing to become pregnant, or by deciding to terminate treatment. Couples may also feel unable to express their own grief because staff disappointment in a treatment failure is so obvious. Mental health professionals can be available both to provide intervention to the infertile couple and to consult with staff who inadvertently might be placing undue pressure on patients. (Reading, 1991: 186)

Couples need to have the time and the opportunity to understand what has happened to the treatment attempt. They need acknowledgement of their feelings of disappointment and frustration from those around them, including family and friends as well as clinic staff. They will then often be in a better position to make a new decision about further treatment, or indeed about ending treatment altogether.

Completing treatment

Useful questions for the counsellor if treatment is completed

- How will they manage the waiting period? What support do they need?
- How do they feel if the treatment does not result in conception?
- What have they learned about the medical and personal processes that may affect future decision making?
- Should the treatment result in conception, how do they now feel? What support do they need now? What are their concerns?

After completion of a treatment programme, the couple then enter into a period of waiting. The counsellors may feel that it is appropriate to help them become aware of what kinds of support they may need during this often difficult and stressful time. If the treatment does *not* result in a pregnancy, the couple are put in the position of needing to decide what further course of action to take. As in cases where treatment has been abandoned, there may now be a sense of hopelessness, as well as anger at the 'failure', at the waste in terms of time, energy and money. Counsellors can help the couple to acknowledge these feelings, and to express their sadness and anger. They are uniquely placed to help the couple make use of their experience to move on positively.

Assertive techniques can be very useful here as Shapiro notes:

> Assertive behaviour . . . has several important dimensions that enable individuals to move from the stage of disorganisation to a stage of reorganisation, which can represent a higher level of functioning. First assertive behaviour enables individuals to identify their own needs. During a crisis, many infertile people are aware of pain and discomfort, but they are less clear about what they need to function more comfortably. With the assistance of the helping professional, the infertile person can acquire a clearer understanding of potential goals for meeting these newly identified needs. Tasks between the infertile person and professional then can be directed toward specific needs that the individual has expressed. Second, assertive behaviour allows the individual to communicate clearly with others. During the period of disorganisation, clarity of communication may have suffered just when the person most needed to have others understand the toll that the crisis had taken. Rebuilding lines of communication, with one's needs clearly in mind, is an important step for the infertile person to take. Third, assertive behaviour enables individuals to respond straightforwardly to insensitive behaviour, rather than seething with resentment, withdrawing, or exploding with anger. (1988: 29)

The infertile couple may need to learn how to behave assertively, not only with the clinic staff, but also with each other and their families. Counsellors can encourage couples to ask questions, make demands and direct as far as is possible the course, kind and tempo of their treatment. Should they need support in different and appropriate ways within the clinic as well as with each other and with their wider support networks, counsellors can help them to gain it. They can help their clients to draw up lists of questions for the consultant before their appointment, conduct practice sessions using role play and encourage clients to ask for clarification should medical language be too obscure. Clients can be encouraged to ask the purpose, results and significance of any tests. Any other situation that may be causing anxiety, such as the couple telling their parents about their infertility and their desire to use donated gametes, can also be worked through and practised within the counselling session.

The following case example shows the way in which assertive techniques may be used to help clients feel stronger and in greater control of their situation.

Case example

Joan had been having investigations over a period of two years, starting with temperature charts, a series of hormone tests and lastly a laparoscopy, which showed that she had one blocked fallopian tube. She felt that she was being pushed into having IVF treatment when she was not clear about what her chances were of conceiving 'naturally' in the medium term. She felt that she wanted information about what IVF treatment involved, and what the likely process would be. She believed that her partner, family, the GP and the medical staff involved were keen for her to go straight ahead with IVF treatment, and that she had not had the chance to take stock of what all this meant for *her*. She needed time to consider the implications of what the investigations had shown, to grieve for the losses she had already suffered. The interventions of others into her and her partner's plans to have a child had, for her, been particularly distressing. She also needed to mourn the child she had wanted to have already had by this time.

The counsellor's task here was to encourage her to approach the medical staff with a series of questions to which she wanted answers and clarification. She was then helped to ask her partner for more support in specific ways. One example was letting him know that she wanted his help in telling some close friends about their infertility, something that he had been reluctant to do. In an individual session with the counsellor she practised asking him for this support in role play. The counsellor supported her with suggestions and help about the most effective way of asserting her needs with her partner, as follows:

Joan: Can I please talk to you about telling our friends about our infertility? [*She said this while looking down at her hands and twisting her fingers together. She was smiling in an apologetic way and her voice was very quiet.*]

Counsellor: Will you be aware of your body language now? Your head is bowed, your eyes are averted and I am finding you quite difficult to hear. Will you experiment now with raising your head, straightening your shoulders, looking directly at the chair where we

have 'put' your partner and asking again? I suggest that you begin
with something like, 'I want to discuss with you . . .'

Joan and the counsellor went through this several times, changing
the form of words, experimenting with different postures, until Joan
reported that she was feeling stronger and more able to assert her
needs with her partner about this issue.

In a later joint session with the counsellor they, as a couple, were
encouraged to talk directly to each other about their needs regarding these particular friends, and to come to a compromise. Joan
then asserted herself in the way in which she had practised in the
individual session earlier. (See Chapter 8 for a fuller discussion of
working with couples.)

Joan was also encouraged to be assertive with her parents, in
particular her mother, who was apparently anxious to have
grandchildren, and was thus pushing her daughter to pursue all the
medical options available. After a short time Joan began to feel
much more in control, less tearful and generally stronger. She had
felt disempowered, 'blown about like a leaf', by events and by the
way in which others had tried to help, without particularly taking
account of what *she* wanted. Her partner was also experiencing
some of the same feelings and he also needed to be encouraged to
behave more assertively, especially with the medical staff, by whom
he felt sidelined and excluded, since they were concentrating their
efforts on Joan.

The treatment may result in a conception and couples will usually
feel excited and pleased by this. However, even at this point the
couple may have some ambivalence, not only about the pregnancy
itself, but about the process that they have gone through to achieve
it. They may also be experiencing some concerns about leaving the
clinic structure and the support that it has offered them. The
pregnancy represents success, but also loss. This will be more fully
discussed in the next chapter.

Whatever the process that a couple may have gone through and
whatever the outcome, couples and individuals will often experience
feelings of loss, anger and fear, and need help to enable them to
make sense of this experience. Those who are in the middle phase
of having treatment experience 'mini cycles' of loss, and can go
around and around the same cycle, as described in Figure 4.2. The
counsellor's role now is to help them to take the support, time and
information they need so that they can manage this stressful time
most effectively. It is a time when people may experience chronic

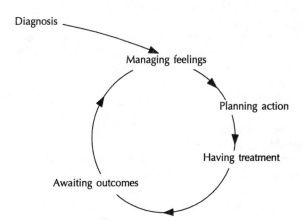

Figure 4.2 *The ICM showing 'mini-cycles' of loss*

grief. They are through the first shock of the diagnosis, and are into what may be a long process of treatment, disappointment, treatment, disappointment – the 'roller-coaster' effect mentioned earlier.

> Couples who are most likely to experience chronic grief are those with unexplained infertility. These infertile people probably have already experienced the stages of acute grief, but they are not able to achieve the final stage of acceptance; their infertility represents a partial loss rather than a final one. Some couples actually admit that it would be far easier if a doctor could tell them that they will never give birth to a child, because this news would allow them to get on with their lives and the decisions that have been on hold for so long. Others doggedly pursue treatments, feeling that they cannot move beyond their infertility until they have done 'everything possible'. (Shapiro, 1988: 34–5)

It is part of the counsellor's role, as discussed earlier in this chapter, to face the clients with the reality of what is happening, the chances of their achieving pregnancy, and the cost of the pursuit of pregnancy for their relationships, as well as financially and emotionally. Counsellors need to allow the time, and sometimes need to encourage the couple into taking the time necessary, to make this assessment. Counsellors may also find themselves in the position of advocating this need in the face of some opposition or confusion from the medical staff, who may want to continue treatment. Clear aims agreed with the infertile couple for them to pursue, with the counsellor's support, may be a useful way forward here. It may be helpful in the confidential setting of the counselling room to help the couple to clarify their goals, to work out a strategy for their treatment, the form it might take, and the timing of it, so that they can then take this to the consultant or clinic co-ordinator for their views and comments and for any further negotiation. This means that the couple are *proactive* in their relationship to the clinic, and although it may be difficult for the clinic staff at times, it seems to help couples to feel in control, less stressed and distressed during this difficult period. There is a considerable shift in the way in which we now understand the doctor–patient relationship, and it would seem that many in the medical profession are much more accepting of this and indeed encourage patients to be assertive and proactive in their treatment programmes. However, patients may not feel that this is, as yet, as easy for them as this would seem, and the counsellor can offer them the support that they may need to make it a reality.

At the end of a treatment attempt couples may have come to a resolution of their childlessness and feel at ease with their lives, readjusted to take account of the fact that they do not have children. They may alternatively feel that they are clear about their decision to have 'one more' IVF attempt. According to Reading

> Just as a gambler feels that the next bet will be the lucky one, so the infertile couple is left with the uneasy feeling that one more try might bring its reward. The hope arising from each new medical breakthrough is a double-edged sword. It offers the promise of success, but also perpetuates the struggle. (1991: 185)

Thus counsellors have the opportunity to assist couples at this point in their lives to make clear decisions for themselves. This may consist of helping the couple to assess their current feelings and needs regarding their infertility. It may be that the couple need to be allowed to feel that it is legitimate to take time away from the stresses imposed by treatment. It is within the counsellor's role to help them to do this.

Case example

Alison stated that she felt very strongly that she could get pregnant, given the chance, and that she would go on until she had. The counsellor asked if there was any point at which she would end her quest for a child. Alison replied that she had thought that this would be when she had gone through her menopause, but that now that it was possible, using donated ova, to have a child after the menopause, she saw no reason not to continue. She said that she was a little uncomfortable about this and that she had felt that stopping at the 'natural' end of her reproductive life was more sensible and a relief. However, faced with the reality that she had not yet conceived, she was having a great deal of trouble facing the pain of her childlessness and saw the new techniques as offering further hope.

Here the counsellor's role was to work with Alison to help her to face her loss. This was not necessarily with the goal of dissuading her from treatment, but with the aim of giving Alison a chance to assess the impact of her infertility on herself, to gain insight into the cause of her denial and of her desperation at the lack of children and to help her 'test reality' about the chances of her conceiving now. It would entail some 'straight talking' about the statistics, working with her to assess the cost of continuing with treatments as against the cost of ending the search (the loss of her role as a mother, and of the children she had so much wanted), and turning her energies to new and different activities.

A useful technique in cases such as that of Alison is to have the client take each side of their situation and to articulate their feelings and their thoughts about the benefits and losses on either side. This can be a useful way of facilitating decision making. The counsellor could work with a client to examine their thoughts and feelings about the pros and cons of continuing or ending treatment in the following way:

Counsellor: Alison, will you place your thoughts and feelings about continuing with treatments on to this chair here and your thoughts and feelings about ending the treatments altogether onto that one over there? I'll give you a moment to do this. Now, will you go to the first chair and tell me what you are thinking and feeling now about continuing treatment?

Alison: [*moves to the first chair*] I feel so tired, *exhausted*, when I think about going on, it seems too much. Financially it's OK, although I can't do as much travelling as I'd like now because of all this. Timewise it's difficult to think ahead with my work because I don't know what I'll be doing. What if I get pregnant next time? I can't make promises to people about work.

Counsellor: Now will you move to the other chair, and speak from that position?

Alison: [*moves to the second chair*] What a relief! I don't have to worry each cycle, or think about taking the drugs. I feel so sad though.

> *Counsellor*: Alison, you seemed different in each position. In the first you *sounded* and *appeared* exhausted and anxious. In the second you sounded very sad but lighter and less torn apart. What does this mean to you now as you reflect on this?

This brief scenario shows the way in which this strategy may help in the clarification of thoughts and feelings and lead to decisions about the future.

Essentially, the abilities of the counsellor are turned to the task of helping the infertile person to redefine the notions of success and failure. The use of assertive techniques, positive encouragement and the willingness and ability of the counsellor to manage expressions of powerfully painful feelings are all important here.

Working with one person's experience of loss

For the rest of this chapter we will concern ourselves with Zoe, introduced in Chapter 2, who is now in the process of assessing the impact of her infertility on not only her perception of herself as a potential mother, but also her sense of herself as a nice, sensible person who coped very well with most things. The losses that she faced were to do with her self image, her role as a woman and her relationship with her partner, as well as the grief for the child(ren) she had not had and may never have. Zoe was feeling stuck and hopeless in her situation, unsupported by those around her, as well as believing that she *should* manage better by herself than she seemed currently able to do.

> *Zoe*: People just don't seem to be able to say 'I care about you as you are.' They always want to *do* something, or say something that hurts. It's a horrible feeling because I just feel I'm breaking away from lots of people. [*Weeping.*] I phoned one woman, whom I hadn't seen for a long time and said I've been a bit upset because this [the infertility] has been happening, and she said 'Oh now I've got two children I can understand how you feel,' and I thought I don't believe this, all around me people are saying that and then I just don't want to see them, and I say I'll phone them, but I just don't. I need to have people around me friends, it feels horrible . . . [*weeping*].
>
> *Counsellor*: You're feeling really lonely, are you?
>
> *Zoe*: Yes, I do. I feel as if they're all on the other side of the fence. Feels really strange. I think that that's what's frightening me, that I feel like this, so much. I mean I do pull myself together and I'm OK, and friendly and whatever with people in a superficial way, but they feel so distant to me. What's going to happen? Is it always going to be like this?
>
> *Counsellor*: When you are lonely and feeling out of control, you are angry, and all of that makes sense. This seems to touch on your own

issues, of being heard and seen for who you are, being loved for just you, not for all those other things, just for you. These are also all the things you want to give a child. These seem to be the things you feel the lack of now.

Zoe is unambiguously stating her need to be allowed to *be*. In other words, she is wanting to be fully accepted by those close to her. This would mean that they would not be afraid of her pain and her sadness, and would allow her expression of these feelings. She is frustrated and distressed by their need to be active on her behalf, and to give advice. These attempts by her family and friends and by her partner leave her feeling depressed at their lack of understanding. Her desire for acceptance of her feelings is frustrated and instead she feels that she has had to protect them against her pain. This is a common experience for those who are bereaved, who are dealing with life threatening conditions or who are infertile. The counsellor is in a position to allow Zoe to have and experience these feelings and must resist the temptation to divert attention from this expression. The repetition in the counselling session of Zoe's experience outside of it would further suppress the appropriate, necessary and painful exploration of her feelings. This can be difficult for the counsellor since the task may take several sessions and leave the counsellor, too, feeling stuck and helpless. The skill of staying with the feelings of grief, without becoming swamped by them, is an essential one for the counsellor to develop. We now see how the counsellor works with Zoe to help her to make sense of her feelings and to allow Zoe to have the room to express them as fully as she can.

Zoe: [*Sigh*] I just wish . . . I think I thought it would start to get easier, but it just doesn't. Two and a half years. I know it's probably such a short time compared to other people, but it seems such a long time, I would have thought that it would have started to get easier. I just feel that I need to cry and cry and cry, I seem to cry really easily.

Counsellor: You cry really easily . . .?

Zoe: Yes. I'm wondering, what direction do I go in? I know that I can't carry on like this. Perhaps I'm running away, I feel I want to get away from it all. I feel it might destroy my relationship with John.

Counsellor: So you're feeling that your avenues are blocked in many directions, and that the route that you wanted, to have a child, is not happening, it's not happening easily, it's not happening at the moment. That and the fact that perhaps until this last week, you have also felt that its up to you to keep the structure that you have, is all stressful for you.

Zoe: Yes, very much so.

> *Counsellor*: It seems that you've felt that you haven't even had the room to look and see which avenues might be possible. The life direction that you wanted, to have a child, that's not happening, an alternative has been closed down, and so you feel restricted in the house, in the relationship with John.
>
> *Zoe*: Yes. That's how it feels.
>
> *Counsellor*: You don't seem to feel that you can use your creative energies.
>
> *Zoe*: No. I don't know what direction to be going. I feel I do want to get out of that, I do feel that I want to start to do something. I feel sort of blocked off.

The counsellor is examining a deeper empathic understanding of Zoe's experience (Egan, Stage 2), and Zoe seems to be gaining sufficient energy from the process of being heard in this way to make statements of desire to move forward. Had the counsellor been drawn into trying to solve Zoe's problems by making suggestions at this point, Zoe's attention and energy may well have been taken up with resisting these and feeling misunderstood. The counsellor then moves on to explore Zoe's fear of the power of her feelings.

> *Counsellor*: What I understand is that you were frightened at the intensity of what you felt.
>
> *Zoe*: Yes, I was. I was frightened at how angry I was. It was also the thoughts I was having. Thinking that this is just not like me at all, how am I going to cope with this for the rest of my life? That it would be easier if I just wasn't here. I mean I'm not suicidal or anything, but to actually start to think like that, and to think that it would just feel easier just not to be here, but if it's going to be like this all the time, then what's the point? It frightens me to feel like that, it's so negative, just not me. [*Crying.*]
>
> *Counsellor*: It is part of you. It's not you, it's part of you. [*Counsellor stays with the feelings here, and is also confronting Zoe's definition of her* whole *self as negative.*]
>
> *Zoe*: It's not the way I normally feel, I don't give up, I'm usually happy about the world, usually positive about the future, but that seems to have gone. I think that's what frightened me. I suppose it makes sense to be angry, I suppose maybe it's OK. It's also feeling I was out of control.

Zoe seems here to have allowed herself to accept that it is appropriate to feel angry. She is now ready to look ahead a little and to explore her feelings about her future.

> *Counsellor*: It seems difficult to see a future.
>
> *Zoe*: It is . . .
>
> *Counsellor*: . . . and to work constructively for it.

Zoe: Yes. I've just lost interest in everything . . . the future. I don't feel a great enthusiasm to do anything. I keep thinking that that's probably because my energy's really low.

Counsellor: The message that I'm getting loud and clear is that you have come to the end of a particular phase. You've done your degree, you put an enormous amount of creative energy into it, and other directions now are not easy, are not possible, or are different from the ones that you want. So at the same time as you are tired from the work that you have been doing, it seems that you are also tired of feeling that you are having to cope, and are angry with John about that.

Zoe: I'm just tired of trying to pretend to people that I can cope.

Counsellor: I've got this picture of you, having come through a lot of 'stuff', and suddenly in front of you there is this space, and roads in front of you, but they're blocked, things are closing down, and I'm not surprised that there is a sense of panic about that.

Zoe: Yes, that's what it is. [*Crying*.]

Counsellor: And I'm not surprised either that you are furious and raging. You are managing many disappointments at the moment. You are very loyal to John; however, I sense a fair level of disappointment with him.

Zoe: Yes.

Counsellor: Whatever happens between you and John, things have changed in your feelings towards him, you have had to make an adjustment in how you view him and your relationship together and that seems very painful, and may be quite scary. So many of your structures have gone or changed, your expectations of what you were going to be doing have changed. Your expectations of the future, the structures that you have had in the past, that you had relied on, are not solid anymore. And it feels like you are standing in the desert with the wind howling all around, not knowing which way to go, not having a direction, fairly bleak whichever way you go.

Zoe: Whichever way . . . yes . . . .

The counsellor has been working with Zoe through the pain of her losses (Worden Task 2, and Kubler-Ross Stages 2 and 4), acknowledging both her sadness and her anger with her situation as well as the fear of her apparent loss of control over it. The counsellor has been using Egan's Stage 1 skills of paraphrasing and summary as well as the Stage 2 skills of communicating empathic deeper understanding, thus helping Zoe to move through to begin to focus on what strengths she has. The counsellor now begins the task of containing Zoe's feelings, and encouraging her firstly to take care of her own needs.

Counsellor: It is really important now that you find ways of taking care of yourself. You don't need to choose a direction right now, you need to conserve your energies right now, to build strength, and wait until things become clearer and you choose which direction to move.

Zoe: It's just being able to stay with it [*crying*]. I think in a funny sort of way, I have thought about how I survive in this. I've been starting to take good care of myself, and go swimming. I'm starting to stop doing things that I don't want to do.

Counsellor: Good.

Zoe: I've been looking at my diet and everything, now I've got more time I've been more careful about that, and in a small sort of way trying to look after myself. I think that's why it hurts so much when people like my friend says things about my diet, and my weight and everything, as though I'm anorexic. It's so upsetting, I've never been anorexic, just skinny! It's not up to her to diagnose things, it's so personal.

Zoe is again here expressing appropriate anger at the imposition of another's opinion on her.

Zoe: I think I lost weight doing my degree. I wasn't not eating, I was just wound up. A few people have said to me about my weight, and I really want to find a good way of replying to them. Better than 'Fuck off'. [*Laughing.*]

Counsellor: That seems a fair response in the circumstances!

Zoe: Yes. I just want to get a sense of the power back in me to respond. So that I can find the right things to say and say them.

Zoe has found the energy to begin to think about how she might manage these difficulties *for herself*.

Counsellor: So where do you think you are with the fertility issues now?

Zoe: I don't know. I was thinking about that, this whole fertility thing is still there. I've been talking to more people about it. But I feel that I'm working other things through. I feel that other things around me are becoming important. I'm still at the stage where I haven't pursued any options about fertility treatments, I just don't feel I've got the energy to go through that whole process. I just can't.

Counsellor: One of the things I'm aware of is that you seem to be examining your environment. I'm not sure that the infertility *is* taking a back seat at the moment. It's almost as if you're looking at John, your creative energies, the degree, your work . . . all of those are important in themselves but they're also linked to support, what you can get for the infertility side of things . . . whether they are good enough compensations for not having a child.

The presentation of an alternative view to Zoe is one of the skills of showing a deeper empathic understanding towards her and seems to strike the right note with her.

Zoe: Maybe you are right. I haven't thought of it like that but that seems right.

Here the counsellor has helped Zoe to draw together the different strands of her distress about her infertility, and allowed Zoe's expressions of outrage, and of sadness. It was important that the counsellor stay with Zoe's distress and allow Zoe to express herself, so that the counsellor's interventions could then be heard more effectively by Zoe. Then the counsellor was able to draw a picture for Zoe of the 'desert place' that she seemed to have reached. Zoe's ready acknowledgement of the feelings that she experienced in this place allowed the counsellor to help her to see that she did not have to move away from this place but could stay there to gain strength, and to await from within herself the clues that would lead her to take further charge of the direction in which she wanted to go. The acceptance of Zoe's feelings, the way that the counsellor was able to stay with Zoe, and not try to reassure her about the future, allowed Zoe to feel that she was real in her pain and that she would survive it.

This is the main part of the work at this part of the process. It can be very difficult for the counsellor, since it is easy to feel as helpless as the infertile person at times, and it is sometimes very tempting to try to reassure them, to tell them what they want to hear. It is important that counsellors help the couple or individual to work through to *their own solutions*.

5

Facing the Future

Broadly speaking there are two main ways in which treatment ends. First, the infertile couple conceive, and thus treatment is no longer required, and secondly, there is no conception and treatment is deemed unlikely to be 'successful'. Therefore a decision to end treatment must be faced.

When pregnancy occurs

In the first case, it is important to note that although conception has taken place, issues of loss may still be relevant. The couple must make an enormous adjustment in their image of themselves, both as individuals and as a couple. Where they have felt excluded from the rest of the (fertile) world, they are now included, and this may be difficult for them. They will lose the structure that came from being involved in the infertility clinic, and the support of the clinic staff. Relationships that may have developed over many months or even years will change and come to an end. Thus joy may be tinged with sadness and apprehension.

Importantly, issues and concerns that were, until now, 'theoretical' are now real and must be confronted and managed. What do they tell parents and other family members about this pregnancy? How do they both actually feel now that she is pregnant using donor sperm or donor eggs? How does this affect what they wish for the future child and its knowledge or ignorance of its origins? There may also be worries that the couple had suppressed until now, such as fears about whether, as a result of the treatment, there is a higher risk of abnormality, or whether a child will have difficulties adjusting to the knowledge that it was 'conceived' in a glass dish in a laboratory, or using frozen samples from a cryo-preservation tank. The counsellor will need to be prepared to help the couple to understand their fears, and what these concerns might indicate. There may be a sense of guilt or shame which now surfaces about what they have done to have a child. There may also be a sense of guilt about having conceived when so many others at the clinic have not.

Pregnancy and childbirth can be stressful events for any person or couple. For those who conceive after a period of infertility there may be further stresses that need to be understood and managed. The couple may find that they do not feel as united in the actuality of pregnancy as they did when they were standing together facing infertility. The pregnancy may for some bring home the essential difference between the couple, that one is fertile and one is not. The counsellor has an essential role to play in helping to surface and resolve this more difficult and painful side of the 'successful' end to treatment. It is necessary, however, to take care not to 'pathologise' what may be ordinary, everyday concerns involved in the adjustment to pregnancy and approaching parenthood. The counsellor can help the couple to engage in 'reality testing' with others who are also pregnant. It may be reassuring for a couple who have conceived with some form of infertility treatment to find that others who have conceived 'normally' feel similar anxieties and feelings about pregnancy, childbirth and childrearing as they do. Obviously the couple's ability to do this will depend on how much they have felt able to be open about their fertility problems and on the decisions they have made regarding what the child will know about its origins.

Occasionally, the pregnancy brings a couple's deepest fears and conflicts to the surface. These conflicts may have been well hidden, with nothing very obvious to indicate that the couple's relationship is in trouble. There may, however, have been hints that there are problems, such as continual absence from discussions or from treatments of the partner or spouse, or the display of over-controlling behaviour by either one in the couple.

Once the pregnancy is a fact, rather than a hope or a fantasy, the way in which the problems have been managed between the couple may be challenged and break down. The reality of their situation becomes clearer to them. It is at this point that a decision may be made to terminate the pregnancy. This is an unusual occurrence, but one which many counsellors may find distressing. Any counsellor who is in the position of working with a woman or couple in such a position will need to clarify the circumstances carefully and sensitively.

Case example

Letty, aged 35, was in a relationship with Daniel, also 35 years old, who had had a diagnosis of severe oligospermia. After much discussion, they had decided to have IVF. After an attempt using Daniel's sperm, when there had been no successful fertilisations, Letty had wanted to take the specialist's advice and attempt an IVF treatment using donor sperm. Daniel had initially been unhappy about this, finding it difficult to reconcile his belief that Letty loved him, with her desire to have a child, if it wasn't his genetically. He had felt that if she loved him then having 'another man's child', would be impossible for her. They had apparently resolved this between them, and had gone ahead with treatment. At the second IVF attempt, Letty conceived and was delighted. Two months later, Letty contacted the clinic counsellor to say that she needed to have an abortion. In the counselling session that followed, Letty reported that she and Daniel had been having relationship difficulties for some time, and that she had put him under considerable pressure at home to agree to the use of donor sperm. She had felt her 'biological clock' was running, and that a child would help them to repair the problems in the relationship. They had sought relationship counselling in the past, but had not told the clinic counsellor of this since they were afraid that it would jeopardise their chances of acceptance onto the programme. (This would not have been the case. However, it may have alerted the counsellor to their relationship problems.)

Daniel had told Letty four weeks after the pregnancy was confirmed that he couldn't continue the relationship with her, and that he didn't want to be responsible for the care of this child. He left the joint home shortly afterwards.

Letty, although very distressed and angry, had initially determined to continue the pregnancy and manage on her own, with the support of her family and friends. However, she was now feeling completely unable to cope with the thought of what single parenthood would mean. The difference between her 'ideal', that is, a baby with Daniel, the image of a happy family, and the spectre of financial hardship, loneliness and stress, was too much for her to bear and she decided on a termination of her pregnancy.

Such cases are rare, but the potential for such a scenario should be borne in mind when a counsellor is working with a couple who may be in relationship difficulties. The paradox that a counsellor must work with is that the couple who present as united and apparently in harmony may be in as much difficulty as the couple who are more actively and obviously in conflict.

Useful questions for the counsellor

- What concerns do you have now that you are pregnant?
- How has this affected you both so far? Both as individuals and as a couple?
- What difficulties if any, do you now foresee, concerning your families and friends? How will they/do they respond to this news?
- What further thoughts do you now have about whether to tell the child the manner of its conception?

It may be that some couples will need extra reassurance and support as they leave the clinic setting and move into the 'fertile' world that they have been striving to reach for so long. It is the responsibility of the counsellor to ensure that the couple have access to appropriate resources, self-help groups, associations, counselling or therapy as needed, that will help them to make this adjustment.

Some couples may need help to assure themselves that after all they will be adequate parents. Lack of self esteem, of a belief in their own capabilities, is characteristic of some couples who have gone through the process of fertility investigations and treatments. However, research from the City University, London, has shown that 'the quality of parenting in families with a child conceived by assisted conception is superior to that shown by families with a naturally conceived child' (Golombok et al., 1993: 14, 17–22).

It may be helpful to encourage couples to assess the strengths they have found in themselves that have enabled them to get as far as they have, as well as to acknowledge the areas they have found most difficult, and encourage them to get support for these.

Case example

The following example shows the responses, concerns and feelings of Louise and Peter, who have conceived after several cycles of DI.

Counsellor: What is it that you want to discuss today?
Louise: Well, I think we should say that it seems that I'm pregnant.
Counsellor: Congratulations!
Peter: The thing that seems so odd to me is that we've planned for it and not planned for it. That we've always had two levels, I suppose I will have until it's kicking and screaming.

Louise: There is an instant recognition that this has completely changed our lives. It is really surprising how fundamentally different I feel about what is going to come. Even in all sorts of quite practical ways, as well as wondering how it affects our dynamics. I feel very positive about it. There is a bit of ambivalence about the whole idea of pregnancy and the parasitic element I suppose, but I'm quite happy to confess those and take them in my stride, I guess. Basically it's wonderful. [*Laughter.*] Even if it doesn't go all the way through, I know that that would be very sad. I still would have preferred to have got this far even it doesn't go all the way. I told the clinic. They were very pleased. I spoke to the nurse who is new there and did the insemination. Judging from her reaction it is her first pregnancy! [*Laughter.*]

This highlights an important point that some patients/clients articulate, which is that sometimes they are not sure 'whose baby it is'. The clinic staff do invest a great deal in the person's or couple's 'success', and when there is a pregnancy, some people find that they feel that the clinic have claimed the 'success' as their own. There seems to be confusion between pleasure at the outcome, and a sense of '*we* did it' on behalf of the staff. This can be discomfiting for the individual or couple, and in some cases increase their sense of distance from the whole process.

The counsellor now moves on to explore the implications of Peter and Louise's news further.

Peter: It's very hard to take in.
Counsellor: Well it's new information and maybe it will take a few weeks before you . . . [*here Louise interrupts*]
Louise: Trust it . . . That's certainly part of it.
Peter: It is hard to believe.
Counsellor: It seems that you are having difficulty in believing this and trusting . . . [*Louise interrupts*]
Louise: That it will remain. I *am* excited about it and I'm determined to enjoy it, even if it doesn't go through, because that's one thing I have learned through all of this, there is nothing wrong with enjoying *now*, then if it goes wrong then it goes wrong and we cope with that then. I've spent so much of my life taking away from my enjoyment of life by being too scared to enjoy things, worrying about the future. I'm determined not to do that, I don't have to do that any more.
Counsellor: It seems a shame to do that doesn't it? This baby deserves to be enjoyed from the beginning.
Louise: Yes! Exactly.
Counsellor: I'm very, very pleased for you both.
Louise: Good, thank you. I feel that you are a part of this too.
Counsellor: Thank you. I appreciate that. Now, what do you need now from me, in the light of this?
Louise: I don't know yet.

Peter: For me there is a 'what to expect' exercise, which we can do from books, but anything that is likely to happen in the next couple of weeks would be useful. And now that we don't have to think about things like IVF, and DI, it brings the focus back to sex and communication between us.

Counsellor: So that is your agenda?

Peter: Yes.

Counsellor: What about you, Louise, what are your needs now?

Louise: I think I'd like to ensure that Peter as well as me has a good say about *this*, I suppose [*indicating abdomen*], that there are ambivalences or difficult things as well as the positive, and that we both have a chance to talk about those. Then the main thing is to do what we are doing now which is to work out what we want to do next. I certainly think that the sex and relationship side need to be continued with at some stage.

Counsellor: So let's look at the ambivalent feelings and fears, so that you acknowledge some of those aspects of what the pregnancy means. Is there any thing else?

The first few minutes of the session have been spent taking in the news, and this includes the counsellor's encouragement to feel the excitement that they have, to identify themselves as potential parents in reality, and to accept the congratulations that any couple in this situation would receive. The counsellor then moves on to helping the couple clarify their needs in relation to this news. Peter seems to be ready to move straight ahead with other concerns, almost as if, for him, he has been able to 'tick off' the pregnancy as 'goal achieved, let's get on with the next problem on the list'. It would be a mistake for the counsellor to follow this, since in the ICM, time needs to be given to the process of Managing Feelings. Therefore, the counsellor chooses to take up Louise's desire to stay with the pregnancy and to explore the fears and ambivalences associated with this. Peter may be unaware of his own feelings about the pregnancy and what this may mean for him, and he seems to be dealing with this by going into 'management' mode.

The counsellor then moves on to facilitating Peter and Louise in the expression of their fears and feelings about the pregnancy.

Counsellor: What are your particular concerns, Louise, about the pregnancy and how it will affect you and your relationship with Peter?

Louise: I think the main thing will be our relationship and what I would like is for you, Peter, to continue expressing how you feel about it and not to be overcome by it all.

Louise is now expressing concern about Peter's response and is needing reassurance that he will be able to take care of his own feelings and thus be in a position to help her adjust to this change in their lives. The counsellor is facilitating them in their expression to each other of their concerns, and encouraging clear communication between them. This is done with the goal of helping them have the capabilities necessary to accommodate the shift in their circumstances that the pregnancy represents.

When treatment ends

Ending treatment may be a decision that is taken by the clinic staff for various reasons, such as that there is no more that can be done, or that the person is unlikely to conceive or that an age factor comes into play. Alternatively, this is a decision that the individual or couple comes to.

A useful way of conceptualising the process of ending is quoted by Shapiro (1988: 122) from Dauten's book, *Quitting: Knowing When to Leave.*

1   Realization of failure: a definitive recognition that events cannot change or be changed.
2   Awareness of the future: an understanding that the future will not bring change and increasing openness to new alternatives.
3   Selfishness: increasing self interest in altering one's situation.
4   The clean decision: taking control of the above three elements and acting on alternatives with some certainty.

Recognising that events cannot change is perhaps the hardest part for those who face childlessness. If, after months or years of striving for a child through one form of assisted conception or another, there is still no pregnancy, then this realisation may be very difficult to come to terms with. However, if the individual or couple has been able to take the time to understand their feelings, to express them in appropriate ways, and to acknowledge their disappointment and pain, then the recognition of the 'end of the road' for them may be more easily arrived at. Acknowledgement early in the process of the emotional, financial and physical costs of the treatments will mean that couples are more likely to recognise when they must stop. If there has been no such acknowledgement then the prospect of ending the search carries with it the suppressed anger, pain and disappointment of all the 'failures'. A useful metaphor for this is of a dam, where unless the sluice gates are opened occasionally to allow the pressure to be relieved, then the pressure builds up and the dam wall cracks and breaks with destructive power.

From the recognition that the situation will not change comes an awareness of the future. Many couples experience a sense of 'time on hold'. Everything is waiting for the baby they hope to have. When couples finally accept their childless state they can then begin to look forward, to explore and be open to other options for themselves. Following on from this comes an increasing focus on recreating their lives in a meaningful way. Finally, there will be action, the couple will make the changes that are needed, and will move forward more firmly and clearly along their chosen path.

These four elements are, in a sense, a detailed formulation of Kubler-Ross's Stage 5, the Acceptance stage, as well as Worden's Task 4, to emotionally relocate and move on. Egan's stages of Exploration, New Understanding and Action are all relevant here.

The couple or individual may, as discussed earlier, cling to treatment, even in the face of overwhelming evidence that this is unlikely to achieve their goal of a pregnancy. The distress that this causes may seem easier to bear than the anxiety provoked by the thought of ending altogether.

The following questions may help the counsellor to elicit the responses that the couple, and the individuals within it, may have to the final ending of treatment.

Useful questions for the counsellor

- What has brought you to this decision now?
- How do you, as individuals and as a couple, feel about this?
- What regrets do you have about this now?
- What has been positive about this whole experience?
- What support do you have or need to help you over the next few weeks and months?
- What are your feelings now, as you look to a future without children?

Case example

Nada and Ahmed, whose issues were looked at in Chapter 3, were refused further treatment by the hospital, who had decided that four IVF attempts were sufficient and wanted to be able to offer the service to those who were more likely than Nada to conceive. The couple had then been referred for ovum donation to another unit. This had been hard for them to accept, since they both had strong feelings about having their own biological child. They also seemed to feel at a loss, having to get used to another clinic and make new relationships with clinic staff. There was also hurt and barely expressed anger at the previous unit 'giving up' on them, and not offering them 'hope'. This example shows how difficult it is for a couple to accept a decision that has been made for them. It demonstrates the counsellor's task, which is to allow the time to acknowledge feelings of anger and frustration, as well as of grief, so that the couple can move forward to further decision making more assertively.

> *Nada*: Obviously everybody would like their own child, but having donor eggs is better than not having, never having any.
> *Ahmed*: For us it would be ideal if we could still go ahead with treatment as before. But now they refuse us. They don't give us any more hope. That is the only reason that we have decided to try another way, another treatment, otherwise we would stay there.
> *Counsellor*: So it seems that not only have you had to consider what having donated eggs means for you, but you are also managing your disappointment about the hospital's decision to stop treating you. Is that right?
> *Ahmed*: Yes, I still don't see why they couldn't have kept going with us. It is so hard to start again.

Although Nada and Ahmed were not yet at the stage of ending treatments altogether, it was still important for them to have the opportunity to express their hurt and disappointment about the clinic's refusal to continue with IVF.

In such cases referral for ongoing help, support, counselling or psychotherapy may be needed, and such resources should be made available. It seems a harder task for the counsellor to help the infertile couple to the point of acceptance of the ending, whatever kind of ending it may be, when it has been imposed on them, rather than if it is a choice arising from their own need. Here the counsellor's task is to allow the expression of anger and again, as in the case of Erica in Chapter 4, to face the couple with the reality of their situation.

Reframing

One of the key skills a counsellor can employ in working with people who are considering the ending of treatment, or of their search for a child, is that of 'reframing'. 'Reframing' the decision to end as a 'success', rather than a 'failure' or a defeat will help the couple to move forward with the understanding that they have chosen to take charge of their lives, to make decisions that have consequences and to take appropriate responsibility for those decisions. This can be done throughout the counselling relationship, and even where the counsellor will see the individual or couple only once.

Case example

Julia and Philip had come to the decision to end treatments, partly due to the financial cost, and partly due to their recognition that their lives were not satisfactory and that they wished to change the way they were living. Philip was, however, having some difficulty in finding the positive side of this decision and, being someone who saw 'success' and 'failure' as measures of effort, was feeling that they had failed.

Counsellor: How do you feel now about ending treatment?

Philip: It all seems such a waste of time and energy, and all for nothing.

Counsellor: All for nothing? I know that you have not had a child but have you got anything from this process?

Philip: Well, I suppose that I've got a lot of knowledge about fertility treatment and how this all works. I guess I also realise that life is not always the way you want it. I'm more sympathetic to others, I think. Basically, though, it's been a failure.

Counsellor: How about you Julia? Is that how you feel too?

Julia: Not so much. I'm very sad that we will not have children but I feel more positive than Philip. I think this whole thing has brought us much closer together. We are much more aware of how each of us is feeling about many things, not just the children thing. In that way I don't regret it at all. I'm glad that we have decided to stop. It's time we looked after ourselves, and did those things that we have been waiting to do, but because of the treatments, haven't done. I'm looking forward to that.

Philip: I feel that way too. But I'm not used to 'giving up', and it does seem that way sometimes.

Counsellor: Perhaps it is important to begin to acknowledge to yourself that you have done all that you can, and that it is not a failure to recognise that. It is a success that you are able to see what is happening and make a choice about that.

Philip: Trouble is, it doesn't feel like a choice that I'm infertile. I see what you are saying though. We can't do anything about that now, and it is a choice to say that we are not going to continue indefinitely paying out financially and what is more important, emotionally, in the attempt to have a child. I'm sad too, but it does feel like the right decision.

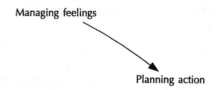

Diagnosis

Managing feelings

Planning action

Having treatment

Awaiting outcomes

Figure 5.1   *The ICM showing Julia and Philip managing feelings and moving on to planning action*

Philip has acknowledged that there are some positives in this experience, although he is still to some extent feeling the sadness and sense of injustice that he is infertile. The verbalisation of this with his wife helps to stop the spiral into anger and depression that could come from staying with the injustice. The counsellor can do this work only when the wife has also acknowledged the reality of the unfairness of what has happened to her husband.

In the terms of the ICM Julia and Philip are at the point of managing their feelings as shown in Figure 5.1. They are now looking outward from the cycle that they have been engaged in, as shown in Figure 5.2.

Julia and Philip still have some way to go before they are able to use most of their energies in looking to the future, instead of grieving for the past. However they have reached a conclusion that seems right for them, and seem to be able to incorporate what has happened and move on – Kubler-Ross's Stage 5 (Acceptance) and Worden's Task 4 (to emotionally relocate and move on).

Grieving
There will be grief associated with the decision to end treatment; grief that may have been avoided while there was 'hope' for a pregnancy. This may emerge very powerfully and seem overwhelming to the couple or individual concerned and will need to be confronted and worked with. As mentioned earlier in this chapter, couples will also be contemplating the ending of their

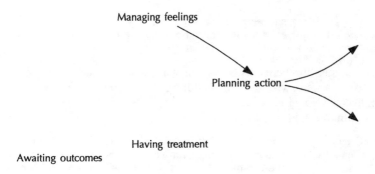

Diagnosis

Managing feelings

Planning action

Having treatment

Awaiting outcomes

Figure 5.2 *The ICM showing Julia and Philip considering alternatives to treatment*

relationship with the clinic staff, with the loss of their support and encouragement.

Case example

Returning to the example of Zoe, whose process was explored in Chapters 2 and 4, it may be helpful to our discussion here to show how she completes her grieving and is at last able to make decisions about her future as a result. After a long period of exploring the implications of her infertility, Zoe decided that she would not continue with investigations or treatment. Initially, Zoe expressed tremendous relief about this and seemed to have renewed energy. However, after a short time, Zoe began to feel enormous sadness, and frequently broke into silent crying, especially when the counsellor confronted her with her loss. It seemed to the counsellor that although the decision seemed appropriate and clear, there was something missing for Zoe, which meant that she had not let go sufficiently. The clue to this was in the manner of her crying. In their book *Healing Pain*, Nini Leick and Marianne Davidsen-Nielsen make a distinction between 'calling weeping' and 'letting go' weeping. 'The calling weeping which Bowlby describes is attempting to hold on to the person or thing which has been lost . . . and it does not bring the same relief as does the deep weeping which occurs when someone begins to let go' (1991: 10). Zoe was weeping in a way that did not bring her deep relief. It was thus the counsellor's task to help Zoe to express her grief fully, to facilitate her in 'letting go'.

Counsellor: What seems hardest for you now, Zoe?
Zoe: I'm just so sad. I'll never have a baby, a child, I had even given names to the children . . . [*crying softly*] . . . I just wish . . .

The counsellor here has a clue in what Zoe has just said. Zoe is talking about wishing for children, for fertility perhaps. This indicates a longing, a yearning, a calling after the lost children. Zoe has not yet said good-bye.

Counsellor: It seems to me that in spite of having made a decision to end treatment that seems right for you, you have not grieved and said a final good-bye to the children that you will now never have. Is that right?
Zoe: It's as though I know that this is the right decision, but I still feel sad. I cry and cry and I don't feel any better.
Counsellor: So your feelings have not 'caught up' with your thinking?
Zoe: That's right.
Counsellor: I wonder if it would be a good idea to look at ways in which you can say a final good-bye to the children you have not had. What do you think about that?
Zoe: It sounds like a good idea, but how? It is not as if they were ever real. I don't have any photos, or clothes. I don't even have a dead baby [*weeping*].
Counsellor: Your children were real to you in your imagination. You had given them names, you had ideas about how they might look, what their personalities might be like. You saw yourself in relation to them. Now you must say a final farewell to these potential children. How do you think you might do that?

The counsellor here is working towards an alliance with Zoe about the nature of the work to be done and is also obtaining her agreement to do the necessary work. This is important if it is to have meaning for Zoe. Note also the counsellor's repetition of the words 'final' and 'good-bye' or 'farewell'. This usage underpins the counsellor's goal of confronting Zoe with the reality of her decision.

Zoe: I'm not sure. When my uncle died, when I was child, I remember that my aunt planted a rose tree in her garden. I remember thinking then that that was a lovely thing to do.
Counsellor: Is that what you would like to do for your children?
Zoe: [*crying*] Yes. I think that would be a good thing to do.
Counsellor: Are you willing to do this?
Zoe: Yes, yes I am.
Counsellor: Do you want John's help with this?
Zoe: I think it would be good if we could do it together. He seems to feel so helpless about it all, although he might think it's a bit silly.

Perhaps it would give him something to do though. Anyway, I want him there. He'll want to be there too.

Counsellor: Is there anything else that you would like to do, or any other way of saying this final good-bye to your children?

Note that the counsellor does not offer comfort at this time, but continues to press Zoe for what she wants in planning this good-bye to her children. This *is* like planning a funeral, and thus must be as personal and meaningful for Zoe as possible.

Zoe: I'd want to celebrate them in some way. All the best funerals, I think, celebrate the life of the person. Although there have been no children, perhaps I could celebrate that I wanted them, that I was willing to do a great deal to have them. Also to celebrate my nurturing and giving side, that I'll now use in other ways.

Here, Zoe has recognised what is happening and has entered into the spirit of the planning of this good-bye event. As in any funeral, the ceremony and ritual involved in saying good-bye is a necessary process for the living. As Worden says, a funeral can 'help make real the fact of the loss . . . give people an opportunity to express thoughts and feelings about the [deceased] . . . be a reflection of the life of the person . . . have the effect of drawing a social support network close' (Worden, 1991: 61–2).

The counsellor then continues the work of facilitating Zoe in managing and expressing her grief.

Counsellor: Great! How do you want to do that?

Zoe: Champagne, and a little speech I think. Something like that.

Counsellor: Good. Perhaps it would be a good idea now to think about what you would like to say, and about who else, apart from your husband John, you would like to be there to share this with you, or perhaps to say something as well.

The session continues from here, going into the details of planning this farewell, exploring what Zoe wants and needs for this occasion to be significant and useful for her. In looking at this seriously, in inviting Zoe to consider this course, the counsellor lets Zoe know that her feelings of loss are real and need to be acknowledged in some formal and even ritualised way. In doing this the counsellor encourages Zoe to actualise her loss, to make it real, and thus to grieve it appropriately and in a healthy way. There are two other strategies for 'actualising the loss' that are worth mentioning here. These are chair work and letter writing.

Chair work The counsellor suggests that the client place their potential child(ren) on a chair, or cushion, in front of them. It is helpful to encourage the client to visualise the child(ren) quite specifically, if possible their hair and eye colour, age, clothes etc. The counsellor then suggests that the client tell the child(ren) what she/he had hoped for from having them in reality, what they would have liked for the child(ren), how they would have wanted to be parents to them. Then the client is encouraged to say good-bye to the child(ren). It must be made clear that this is a final good-bye, that there will be no 'revisiting'. This 'face to face' encounter can be an extremely powerful experience. It is more likely to be used by experienced counsellors and therapists who have had a fairly long-term relationship with the infertile person or couple.

Letter writing   This strategy for actualising the loss that the infertile person may feel is one that has been used both in this context and in working with those who have had a termination of a pregnancy (as indeed has the chair work described above). Here, the counsellor suggests that the person write a letter to their potential child(ren), including in it all their hopes and desires that had been bound up with having children. It is also important to include their fantasy of what the child(ren) would have been, how they would have looked and so on. This letter may be written over several weeks. It does not have to be read aloud, or shared with the counsellor. It may be shared between partners, who may both write letters and thus share their loss in a very powerful way. However, reading the letter aloud, with the partner and counsellor present, may actualise the loss in a more meaningful way, by allowing a 'witness' to the grief expressed.

The decision to end treatment is a very hard one for most couples to make, not just for the reasons mentioned earlier, but also because for some there is a sense of 'giving up', not persevering long enough, and thus there is, for them, a sense of failure. The couple may feel angry that nothing has worked even though they have made every effort and done all that they could. 'Anger and frustration are common, especially among couples who believe that if one tries hard enough and "does everything right," one can expect to achieve life goals' (Shapiro, 1988: 123).

In the case of Julia and Philip discussed earlier, Philip was somebody who had this belief. He was a high achiever at work, working hard all his life, and before he had discovered he was infertile, had expected his life to go according to plan. It was thus a tremendous shock for him when it did not and because of his belief about success he found it very difficult indeed to understand what had happened in any other way than as a personal failure. Part of his process was to express his anger and frustration at his power-lessness to achieve exactly what he wanted, and to come to a recognition that this was not *his fault*. He was then able to begin to use his considerable energies in choosing a different life path.

The counsellor's sensitive acknowledgement of the decision to end treatment is vital. The impulse to hold out continuing hope for 'one more try' when someone is indicating a need to end the search is not only inappropriate but may be damaging in the sense that one of the goals in counselling is to help people to make sense of and take charge of their lives in as much as they are able to do so. To invite them to continue with treatments is to invite them to *please* you as doctor/nurse/counsellor, to continue to *try hard* and to adapt to *your* wishes. Counsellors in particular must be wary of the temptation to placate the client's feelings by encouraging them to continue. There is a fine line between encouraging and supporting the infertile couple or person who is cast down and despairing about the latest 'failure' of a treatment, and recognising that they are beginning, however tentatively, to indicate a need to terminate treatment.

6

Abortion Counselling

In this chapter I want to show how there are many similarities in terms of both the issues and the counselling approach between those who are having problems in conceiving and those who have conceived and are unable or unwilling for various reasons to continue with the pregnancy. The issues of secrecy, control, fear, stigmatisation and the existential questions about purpose in life may all have to be addressed when a woman is faced with making a decision about her pregnancy. These concerns may also be raised for her partner, and how these are discussed and resolved, or otherwise, between them, can be enormously helpful or painful for them. The woman may have to adjust her internal view of the kind of person she is. The strength of feeling about abortion both in Britain and the United States means that many people have particular notions about *what kind of woman* has an abortion. Therefore when a woman is confronted by an unwanted, unplanned or abnormal pregnancy, when she seeks a termination she is also confronted by what may be a very painful readjustment in her self-image. Alternatively, she may go through what may be an equally painful reassessment of her values in order to accommodate this new situation. How deeply these are felt has implications for the amount of conflict the woman, and possibly her partner, experiences, and thus the level and amount of counselling which may be needed.

The overall context in which abortion counselling takes place has been discussed in Chapter 1. It is important for the counsellor to hold in mind the religious, cultural, social and legal context in which a decision about a termination of pregnancy is made. In both Britain and the United States an abortion is a legal as well as a medical procedure, and the counselling process is therefore bound by the constraints that this imposes.

Within these constraints, the task of the counsellor is to help the woman come to a decision about her pregnancy, taking into account her particular circumstances. The focus of the counselling interview *must* be the decision-making process, and the counsellor must be able to guide the session towards this.

Ideally, the process from the point of diagnosis of a pregnancy should include the management of the feelings that this situation raises, before any action is planned or treatment undertaken. Therefore it can be shown that the Infertility Counselling Model (ICM) also applies to those who seek (or need) a termination of pregnancy, as shown in Figure 6.1.

The process of counselling women, and their husband or partner as necessary, about their pregnancy with a view to a possible abortion requires the counsellor to make a rapid assessment of the woman's counselling need. The reality is that for most women the counselling session is a half- to one-hour process and is a once-only occasion. This is because most counselling services for those considering a termination of their pregnancy are organised within one consultation appointment, which means that the counsellor is just one of the people that a woman attending will see. The others include doctors, nurses and administrators. It is therefore necessary that the counsellor is able to judge quickly what the particular issues are for this client.

Useful questions for the counsellor to have in mind

- What was the manner of conception?
- What contraception if any, was used?
- What is the support network?
- Who else knows of the pregnancy?
- What is the involvement, if any, of the putative father?
- What has been the parental response to this situation (in cases where parental consent is required by law)?

The diagnosis, or discovery, of pregnancy may be devastating for some, and the person may respond with shock and denial. This sometimes accounts for the late presentation of some women for help in terminating their pregnancy. Sometimes this will be the case for a woman who is hoping against hope that her husband or partner may change his mind about being willing to have the child; or who through lack of knowledge believes that they could not have conceived as a result of the particular sexual activity that they engaged in; or that the timing of the activity meant that pregnancy was impossible; or who denies to themselves how long ago it was that they missed their period. Some will isolate also themselves and become withdrawn from their families and friends, and are thus even less likely to be

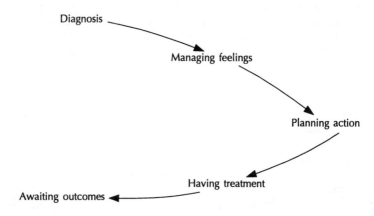

Figure 6.1   *The ICM applied to termination of pregnancy*

confronted by them about the body changes that are occurring. This group of women can be said to be in Kubler-Ross's Stage 1 of Denial and Isolation.

The similarities with someone who has received a diagnosis of a fertility problem are to do with the client's need to take urgent action to deal with the situation. This is particularly the case for an unplanned or unwanted pregnancy, where there is a general belief that the sooner the abortion happens the better. However, there is almost always the time to take a few days to consider the decision carefully. Ensuring that there *is* this time is not an attempt to have the woman change her mind, but rather, comes from an awareness that those women who have allowed themselves to take time over the decision to terminate a pregnancy tend to be better able to manage their feelings after the abortion. Again, as in the situation of someone with a fertility problem, time to consider the implications as well as the feelings associated with any particular course of action is important. There should always be an opportunity for the woman, along with her partner if appropriate, to discuss fears or concerns about the procedure, to ascertain support networks and their use and availability. This time can also be used to examine and express any feelings about the pregnancy and a decision to terminate.

In the United States there is a '24-hour' rule between consultation and the termination of the pregnancy, and this is effectively also what happens in Britain. It supposes that a woman has not considered her options before attending for consultation, which may be the case for some. An important part of the skills that a

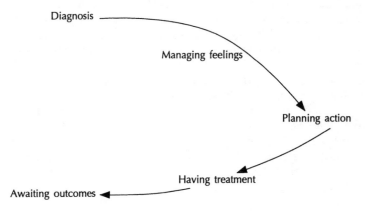

Figure 6.2 *The ICM showing how feelings may be denied when considering termination of pregnancy*

counsellor employs in such an environment is to be able to assess which clients need to be given time to define and express their feelings about their situation further, before having any termination of pregnancy. Some women may feel differently after the consultation and do need further time to consider their options before making a firm decision. However, many women have thought through their situation, considered their options, understood and expressed the feelings that they have about the pregnancy and what it means to them to have an abortion, and merely want a service. A counsellor in such a service must have the skills to work quickly to ascertain which women are in the latter group, and which in the former. Counsellors will need to develop these skills in assessing a woman's situation, in particular *how* she responds to the questions the counsellor puts to her.

Some women respond with panic to a confirmation of an unwanted or unplanned pregnancy. This panic reaction may drive the woman, and those around her, including abortion services, into precipitate action. The counsellor is therefore in the position of encouraging and supporting the woman (and her partner, if needed) to take the time and opportunity to deal with their feelings, in a situation where there is a great temptation to 'hurry up and get it over with'. This temptation can be formulated as shown in Figure 6.2.

It is apparent that the process which a woman goes through in making her decision about her pregnancy is similar to that through which an infertile couple also pass when considering the implications of their infertility on their lives. In both situations the clients confront questions about their role in life; they must deal with the issues that they may have about control; they face questions about the meaning and importance of their relationships; and all of this is within the context not only of a medical procedure, or series of procedures, but also a legal framework in which they and their circumstances must satisfy certain criteria.

A major difference here is that at the stage of awaiting outcomes, rather than waiting to see if fertilisation has taken place, or the embryo implanted, the woman who has had a termination of her pregnancy may be anxious to be sure that the termination has actually occurred, and is free of complications, either physical or psychological.

The counselling process

There are some useful areas to be worked through when managing the counselling session with somebody who is attending for consultation about a termination of pregnancy.

Useful questions for the counsellor

- How did you feel when you first realised that you were pregnant? What was your first reaction?
- Who else knows about your pregnancy?
- How do you feel about having a termination of pregnancy?
- How do you feel about continuing the pregnancy?
- How have you felt in the past about abortion?
- What concerns do you have about the procedure for termination of pregnancy?

The answers to the first question about initial reactions may reveal any ambivalence about the pregnancy. For some, it was clear from the first inkling that they might be pregnant that this was a mistake and there was never a doubt in their mind about allowing the pregnancy to continue. Others may respond differently, suggesting that their first response was one of excitement or pleasure. Further exploration is then needed to discover what in their situation means that they are considering the possibility of an abortion.

The second question about who else is aware that the woman is pregnant will give some indication of what level of support she has. This could include the involvement or otherwise of the putative father, what significance the pregnancy has within the relationship, whether there is an issue about parental involvement, and in general the circumstances in which the woman now has to consider her decision.

The third question may reveal what main areas of concern the woman has about abortion. This may be not that she is pregnant, but that she had sex and that people will now know this about her. The woman may be less concerned about the pregnancy as such, and more anxious that she has in some way lost control of her life, and is in the unwelcome position of needing to involve others in decision making about her situation.

The fourth question may be helpful when working with someone who appears somewhat ambivalent. This question about continuing the pregnancy faces the client with the reality of what a baby and a growing child might mean for her. It also may allow disclosure of her home circumstances, such as strict parents who may be unsympathetic or unhelpful. This could include a fear of condemnation, criticism, rejection, or other, possibly violent, responses from the family, or partner. It may be a cause of the ambivalence, since some women may be torn between the desire to have the child, and in this way have someone who loves them unconditionally and whom they can love, and the need to retain the respect and approval of those around them.

The fifth question, which asks about previous feelings about abortion, can be useful in helping to ascertain whether the client is coming up against a strongly held belief about abortion. Should this be the case, it may be that she must somehow satisfy this value system, and perhaps rationalise her need or wish for an abortion. Some women do this by declaring that they are not like others who seek abortion, that *their* circumstances require it, that they are different. Others may reveal a need to rebel against this belief system, and the pregnancy may be a conscious or unconscious expression of this rebellion. In either case there is need to accommodate these strongly held beliefs so that a clear and appropriate decision is made.

The sixth question is a helpful way of determining whether the woman has fears about the procedure itself. These fears may be about anaesthetic, or its lack, the actual process of the abortion itself, or about the legal and medical procedures through which she must go prior to the abortion itself. This may be the only worry that the client has and the fact that this is a termination of pregnancy is no more important than if it were the removal of a cyst or some other minor medical procedure.

It is important for the counsellor to remain open to the woman's own issues, as always in counselling, since for some there will be no particular conflict, fear or concern about abortion, and their main aim is to have it done properly and with the minimum amount of fuss and delay.

Body language

How a woman responds to questions about her pregnancy may give the counsellor a lot of information rapidly, not only in her spoken replies, but also the *way* in which she responds; how she uses her eyes, and her hands, her general body posture, what she does not reply to as well as what she does.

Case example

This is an example of working with a woman who is clear about her situation and about her decision to have an abortion. Her body language gives the first indication of this. It is important to note that this certainty exemplifies the majority of women who get as far as having a consultation about a termination of pregnancy.

Polly is a woman in her late twenties who is in a long-term relationship with her partner, Mark. She is between 6 and 8 weeks pregnant. Polly enters the room with her head up and her eyes looking directly at the counsellor. She sits down and answers the questions clearly and thoughtfully.

> *Counsellor*: You have come today to discuss the possibility of terminating your pregnancy. Is that right?
>
> *Polly*: Yes, that's right. I knew straight away that this had all come at the wrong time.
>
> *Counsellor*: So you were clear immediately that you did not want, or were not in a position to continue with, the pregnancy?
>
> *Polly*: Yes. My heart sank when I got the pregnancy test result, although I think I knew before.
>
> *Counsellor*: How have you been feeling since you found out that you were pregnant?
>
> *Polly*: Well, I've just wanted to get it over with really. I've talked it over with my partner, Mark, and he's been really great. He was just as upset about it as I was. We both feel that this is the wrong time, he's only just getting the business off the ground, and my career is going well, but it would be a bad time to take maternity leave, I want to be more established with the company. We just couldn't

afford it right now. Anyway, I'm not really sure that I want children at all, and I really don't want a baby at the moment.

Counsellor: So you and Mark are both clear about this decision?

Polly: Yes. As I said we are both upset about it, because we never wanted to be in this position. We are both a bit shocked really, he was using the sheath and nothing seemed to be wrong with it, we haven't had any 'accidents' with it and we always used it. It seems a bit unfair when you are being responsible.

Counsellor: So, can you say what it is that has upset you about all this?

Here the counsellor is picking up on what seems to be an indication of possible ambivalence, and inviting Polly to explore further what the issues are that have distressed her.

Polly: Well it's the unfairness of it, I suppose. It isn't what we wanted, and it *is* a shame, to have to do this. We are clear about it, and I feel better about it as we weren't being irresponsible about birth control.

Counsellor: So it seems unfair, but you feel that it is the right thing for you both at this stage, and you have good support from Mark as well?

Here the counsellor is *summarising* what has been covered so far. This has the effect of showing Polly that the counsellor has heard and understood, as well as gently encouraging Polly to move on with her story.

Polly: Yes, I suppose that's right. My parents have been very understanding and my doctor has been very supportive too. That helps. My doctor has given me lots of information and the whole procedure seems fairly straightforward.

Counsellor: Do you have any concerns about the procedure itself?

Polly: Well, I'm a bit nervous about it. I've never done anything like this, but it seems simple.

Counsellor: Would it be helpful for you to run through the procedure with you, so you know what to expect?

The counsellor might explain the process that a woman goes through before the abortion operation, the abortion itself and post-abortion care in some detail here, as this can later help the woman to feel that she is not surrendering herself to an unknown and frightening experience and therefore that she has an element of understanding and is in control.

Counsellor: Have you ever had any strong feelings about abortion in the past, how have you felt about it?

Polly: Well I've always thought that it should be available for women, I've never had a problem about it, it's something that women have a right to, I think.

Polly shows here that she does not have a conflict between her need and wish for a termination of her pregnancy and her value system. They are compatible and this indicates that Polly is unlikely to suffer from guilt after the abortion and is more likely to integrate the experience of the abortion in a healthy way. It would be helpful to suggest to Polly that should she feel sad about the abortion that she should allow herself to cry and grieve about it. It seems that many women feel that because they have chosen to have an abortion they have in some way forfeited the right to grieve it as a loss. This permission may help Polly to recover more easily from the experience. Polly shows that she has good support, she clearly feels that she can make her own decisions, and is in a low risk group for any emotional and psychological difficulties after the abortion.

As one gynaecologist, quoted in a report on counselling provision, said, 'I'm looking for the woman to make the decision that *at the time* she really has no alternative. It doesn't mean that she won't have regrets, but regrets are relatively small . . . I see very few regrets' (Allen, 1985: 280). In my experience the women who have few regrets are not just those who have come to the conclusion that they have no alternative, but those who have felt that *they* have made the decision, and thus feel in control of events, as well as having good support from partners or husbands, friends and family, and little or no conflict between their decision and their value system.

However, there is an important caveat here. It is not always appropriate to stress autonomy and decision making skills or to make these a goal within the counselling relationship. The understanding that a woman adjusts more easily after an abortion if she has felt some measure of control prior to the decision, and has felt that it *was* her decision, may not apply for certain groups of women whose psychological and physical well-being is dependent on adapting to her husband's or family's pressures to have an abortion. To try to alert these women to the possibility of real choice, or of taking personal decisions that others may disapprove of, is inappropriate. At best this may be confusing for the woman, and at worst it may add to her distress. Whatever the counsellor believes about 'a woman's right to choose', there are occasions such as the ones highlighted above where the counsellor needs to let go of this, and to allow the woman to know what is best for herself within her own religious, cultural or social context.

Case example

The following example shows the process of counselling Amy, a
woman who is to some extent ambivalent about having an
abortion, and is struggling with painful internal conflicts about her
own needs and her role as a wife and mother, as well as a strong
sense of shame, and low self-esteem. Again, the first indications of
this are in her body language.

Amy is 38 years old, is married with three children, now all in
their teens, and is now 10–12 weeks pregnant. She enters the room
seeming anxious and ill at ease, demonstrating this by the way in
which her eyes flicker around the room, and do not make any more
than fleeting contact with the counsellor. Amy 'fusses' with her
coat, and sits down with her hands clenched together on her lap,
her legs drawn up under the chair with the ankles crossed. She
answers the questions that the counsellor puts to her in a
roundabout and nervous way. Amy opens the discussion.

> *Amy*: I hope I'm not going to be very long, I've got to get home
> soon.

The counsellor is immediately presented with a choice of responses,
which include answering at the 'overt' level, and giving information
about the process that Amy needs to enter; interpreting Amy's
behaviour, perhaps by commenting on her apparent nervousness,
'You seem rather nervous, is this very difficult for you?'; or
reflecting her behaviour, 'I notice that you are sitting there with
your hands clenched. Can you tell me what this is about?'

Given the situation in which this interview is taking place, and
that the counsellor and client have only just met, as well as an
understanding on the counsellor's part that many women find this
situation anxiety-provoking, the counsellor here thinks that the
most appropriate response is the first, 'overt' response, and answers
the question 'straight'. However, answering at the surface level will
often also open the door to feelings, as is shown in the next
interaction.

> *Counsellor*: Well, there are some questions that we will need to ask,
> and then you will need to see the doctor, so you will probably be
> about one to one-and-a-half hours here this morning. Is that going
> to be all right for you?
> *Amy*: Yes, but I don't know what you want to know. I mean I can
> have it done soon can't I?

The counsellor working in England, Wales and Scotland is
presented here with a difficult dilemma. The law requires that any
termination of pregnancy must be agreed by two doctors (see

Appendix). It is not lawful for the counsellor to assure Amy at this stage that she can have the abortion done.

> *Counsellor*: Well, you will need to see the doctor before it can be agreed that you have an abortion. You seem quite anxious about all of this. Will you say what specifically it is that concerns you now?

The counsellor is trying here to contain Amy's anxiety, and encourage Amy to verbalise what her difficulties are. This is so that the counsellor has an opportunity to assess Amy's situation and judge what Amy's counselling needs might be. It is already clear that Amy needs to be encouraged to slow down a little. It is likely that this slowing down is also rather uncomfortable for Amy and in fact might create even greater anxiety for her, should she have to confront what is happening for her in her life. None the less, this is what the counsellor must do if he or she is to discover what the issues are for Amy. In England, Wales and Scotland the law requires that women have reasons for having a termination of pregnancy, and this means that the counsellor must seek to clarify these reasons.

> *Amy*: It's very important that I get this all sorted out soon. My husband will be furious if it isn't properly organised as fast as possible.
> *Counsellor*: So your husband wants this sorted out – what about you, how are you feeling about this pregnancy?

The counsellor is bringing the woman into the here and now, into the room, creating the space and the environment for Amy to begin the process of examining her response and feelings about the pregnancy.

> *Amy*: Oh, I don't know. It all seems such a mess. I never thought that I'd be in this position. I'm not like all these young girls, so irresponsible. I've always been so careful. It seems so ridiculous at my age, to be in this situation. I mean my youngest son is thirteen years old. I thought I was way past getting pregnant. It is not as if we ... well you know ... very often.

Here Amy pauses, looking at the counsellor. The counsellor waits a little, and when it seems that Amy is not going to continue, goes on:

> *Counsellor*: You seem to be saying that you are very surprised and shocked to be pregnant and that part of that shock is that you don't have sex very often. You also seem to be worried about what your husband is feeling about this. Is that right?
> *Amy*: Well, yes, we're getting a bit old for that sort of thing, don't you think? Besides, it's a long time since Peter showed any interest in that side of things with me. But he's absolutely furious about it. He

blames me, and I suppose he's right really, I should have known it wasn't safe.

The counsellor must sort out what to attempt to tackle here, since Amy seems to be operating under a number of assumptions and beliefs about her situation, and whose responsibility it is. These assumptions and beliefs are underpinned by her poor self esteem, which is evidenced by her tendency to self blame. The counsellor's task here is to help Amy to clarify the issues for herself, and allow her to find her way to an understanding of these, so that Amy can make a decision for herself and take responsibility for what that decision means for her. The time that the counsellor creates for Amy is already challenging Amy's 'hurry' at the beginning of the session. Those who are in a hurry are often avoiding feelings. If the counsellor and the other staff in the abortion service had allowed themselves to be driven by Amy's anxiety to reassure her about her situation, then Amy may have had the abortion and blamed her husband for it, although it is probable that this blame would have been masked by her own self blame and lack of self esteem and may have resulted in Amy becoming more depressed than before.

The counsellor continues in the following way:

Counsellor: So you blame yourself for the fact that you are pregnant and you say that Peter blames you too. Can you say a bit more about that and how this affects your decision about whether or not to continue with the pregnancy?

Amy: Well, this is all so inconvenient for him. We've got the three boys and they are so expensive. Peter works very hard to supply everything for us all. I ought to be grateful. I hardly ever see him, and now the eldest is at university, and the others are busy too, I never see them either. I suppose Peter is just beginning to see the end of the financial tunnel and now this happens. He can't bear the thought of starting all over again with a baby. I can understand it, I just wish he wasn't so angry about it.

Counsellor: What about you, can you bear the thought of starting over again with a baby, or not?

The counsellor is working to focus on Amy's feelings and thoughts about her pregnancy.

Amy: Oh yes. That isn't a problem for me. I love babies. But it's totally impractical. Most of our friends would be horrified!

Counsellor: You would like to have the baby, is that right?

Amy: Yes, well I think so, it would be hard work, but I've always wanted a girl, and I'm lonely at home . . . [*crying*] doesn't that sound silly?

Counsellor: So having a baby would give you something to work for, and a girl would help you to feel less lonely in a household of men?

There is silence here while Amy struggles with this formulation of what she is presenting to the counsellor.

> *Amy*:   Well it is not going to happen. It is just ridiculous at my age. Peter won't consider it, and I don't know what the boys would think.

Amy has admitted to herself and to the counsellor during this session that she would in fact like to continue with this pregnancy, but has now retreated to the position of being apparently resigned to the fact that to have a child in her situation is impossible. There is perhaps an element here that it is easier to blame herself, Peter and her environment generally for this impossibility, than to confront what appears to be a crisis in her life, about who she is, what her role is now, as well as a crisis in her relationship, about how to be heard, appreciated and involved within the marriage.

The counsellor is not able to work actively with these issues, since this session is likely to be a 'one-off'. It is possible that the counsellor may want to suggest that they meet again before any decision is made about an abortion. This still would not give them room to address the issues and conflicts that seem to be surfacing. It is not only unhelpful, but, I believe, unethical, to probe into Amy's situation in any further depth without an explicit contract with Amy to do this work. The counsellor must limit her or himself to the task of helping Amy to come to as clear a decision about this pregnancy as possible, and to offering appropriate referral for further work should Amy wish this.

> *Counsellor*:   Amy, it seems that on the one hand you are saying that continuing with this pregnancy is out of the question, that Peter would not support this decision, that your friends would not be supportive either, that your sons would be embarrassed and upset by you having a baby now. On the other hand, you are saying that you want to have a baby, that you would like the challenge of it, that if it were a girl you would like that, and that a baby would help you to feel less lonely. This is how it seems to me, having listened to what you say, and it seems important that you are able to come to a decision that is right for you in all of this.

The counsellor is using summary skills here to help both Amy and herself to clarify what the issues are (Egan Stage 1 skills).

> *Amy*:   When you put it like that, I suppose that is the way it seems. Thinking about it now, I guess I've been reacting to everybody else, and not really stopping to think about what it would mean for me to have an abortion. I don't think I've really thought about what having a baby now, at my age would mean either.

Amy has reached a point now within the counselling session where she can explore the issues for herself and hopefully come to some decision that she is able to accommodate reasonably comfortably. This may mean addressing her needs within her marriage and her family, or it may mean that she chooses not to do that, at least for the moment. What is important in this is that she *chooses* and it is the counsellor's role to enable her to reach a point where this is possible.

In this example, Amy may or may not have an abortion. This is not the issue. The issue is that she has been given an opportunity within the counselling session to take *control* of her situation and have an impact on it. This opportunity is often all that a counsellor working within an abortion service can offer, but it is a great deal. It means that the client is helped to be in charge of a situation that often feels chaotic and out of control. As with those who are infertile this element of control helps the clients to manage a difficult situation more effectively and in a more healthy way. Some women ask the question, 'What do *you* think I should do?' or 'What would you do in my situation?' As with any invitation like this in any counselling situation it is important that the counsellor does not allow him or herself to answer this question. A useful response might be, 'I wonder how it would help you if I were to tell you what I would do?' This often opens up the discussion further about the woman's support network and her need for control over her situation.

Further strategies

There are some other strategies that may help the counsellor to work with the women, and occasionally couples, who are requesting a termination of pregnancy. These are also useful for women who may need to seek counselling help after an abortion.

Diary

For those women who seem to be anxious about how they may feel after an abortion, or who are particularly sad about their decision, it is sometimes helpful to suggest to them that they keep a daily diary from the time that they have attended the counselling session, until perhaps two or three weeks, or longer, after they have had the termination procedure done. This diary should include the woman's description of her feelings, her fears and her thoughts about her decision. This may be useful for her should she feel that after all she could have managed to continue the pregnancy, that it would all have worked out differently. When she looks at what she has written at the time of the abortion decision and the operation, it may help her to evaluate what was really happening for her *at the time*; this way of 'reality testing' may help the woman to understand what was happening and to stop feeling so guilty or remorseful about the abortion.

Letter

In the same way as a diary may be helpful for some women when evaluating their situation or dealing with their feelings after an abortion, a suggestion that the woman write a letter to the child that she did not have may help her to say good-bye to the image of the child. A letter may also allow the woman to express her loss more fully, in a way that she may not allow herself to do, or cannot do, before the abortion. The suggestion that the woman has the right to feel the loss of this pregnancy and potential child may be enough in itself to help the woman express and manage the feelings of sadness that she may have. This in turn may allow her to feel less guilty about her decision.

When a termination is recommended by a doctor due to foetal abnormality, many women feel devastated at the idea that they are deliberately ending the life of a baby that has been very much wanted. For the counsellor the issues are akin to those which are raised in bereavement work, and again the ICM is relevant here. As in the case of a woman, man or couple with a fertility problem, this sort of loss may be unseen by the family and social network of the woman and her husband or partner.

Post-abortion guilt may be intense and may not be mitigated by the knowledge that the child may not have been viable, or would have had severe disability. It is sometimes extremely difficult for these scenarios to have any validity for the woman, when she has no image of what the child would really have been like. It may be helpful, if possible, for the woman or couple to have any scan pictures of the foetus to help in making the situation real. It may be possible, depending on the stage of pregnancy when it is aborted, for the parents to see the foetus, and thus help to actualise the loss (Worden's Task 1). The principles of grief work, described in Chapter 2, apply when a woman is seeking a termination of pregnancy and when she may need help with coming to terms with her decision postoperatively.

7

Fertility and Sexual Problems

It is understood that sexual problems may develop as a result of loss, bereavement or other crisis situations such as redundancy or work-related stress. It is therefore unsurprising that *some* of those who have fertility problems will also have sexual difficulties. These sexual problems will *result from* their infertility problems. It is also the case that a proportion of those presenting at infertility units have a sexual problem that *results in* fertility problems.

In a study of infertile couples conducted in 1988, it was found that: 'Of the possible etiological factors evaluated, sexual dysfunction was the primary cause of infertility in five cases (5%)' (Rantala and Koskimies, 1988: 28). This is not a high figure, but it none the less represents a group for whom expensive and potentially stressful infertility investigations and treatment may be avoided.

When working with infertile couples, sex and sexual activity is always in the background of the discussions. People are attending clinics for help with conception, which is usually achieved through sexual intercourse. Thus, any examination of the couple's difficulty in conceiving must include overt and clear questioning about their sexual activity. This should not, however, only be limited to the initial history taking or assessment phase, since sexual problems may develop over the time that the couple are in treatment. It is incumbent on the counsellor to ask the questions necessary to elicit this information throughout their treatment.

The use of language

The difficulties of language are often most marked when helping professionals assess, work with and treat sexual problems in their clients. It is possibly too obvious to say that those who work with sex and sexuality issues need to have a good awareness of their own sexual problems, areas of difficulty and discomfort. The professional needs also to feel at ease asking explicit questions about sexual behaviour and activity. The following are questions that may help in the eliciting and evaluation of the couple's sexual behaviour.

Useful questions for the counsellor to use to elicit information about sexual activity

- How have your fertility problems affected your relationship, including your sexual relationship?
- Has anything changed in your sexual relationship since you have been trying to conceive?
- How would you describe your sexual activity?
- How frequently do you have penetrative sex (that is, penis in vagina sex)?

Clearly, these questions are explicit, and may embarrass some patients/clients, as well as some professionals. The *way* in which these questions are asked is all-important. If the questioner is relaxed, clear and comfortable, then the clients are likely to be so also. There are occasions where asking such questions may cause offence, and in these cases it may be helpful to remind the couple gently that the questions are an attempt to ascertain whether there are any other problems that might be contributing to their infertility. Additionally, clients often *expect* to be asked explicit and direct questions, and are not usually upset or offended by them. This may be due partly to the medical or office setting where this occurs, which may give the clients a sense of safety and legitimacy.

Sexual problems as a result of infertility investigation, treatment and management

The stress of infertility and its treatment may be a fundamental cause of a variety of sexual problems and difficulties. Male problems may include retarded ejaculation (where a man has difficulty ejaculating intra-vaginally or at all), erectile problems, premature ejaculation (where a man has little or no control over his ejaculatory response, and where he may ejaculate before vaginal entry is achieved), or loss of desire, with a consequent decrease in sexual activity. Female problems may include loss of desire, anorgasmia (no orgasm), dyspareunia (painful intercourse), vaginismus (the involuntary spasm of the vaginal muscles) making intercourse or vaginal examination impossible, and which may occur secondarily as a response to pelvic pain or painful intercourse.

The counsellor must be aware that these sexual difficulties may be present in the couple and must be prepared to ask about their clients' current sexual activity at regular intervals throughout the investigation or treatment processes as well as their feelings and concerns regarding it. Sexual problems, as I have said, may be caused by the feelings that an individual experiences during the investigations and the procedures undertaken in the effort to overcome their infertility. These may be the direct physical results of medical procedures, such as pain on intercourse (dyspareunia) following pelvic surgery or examination, which may then linger in the client as a fear response when the original cause of the pain has disappeared.

Men may find that the process of providing semen samples to order affects their ability to gain and to maintain an erection. The surroundings in which men are expected to do this may be far from ideal, perhaps at best warm although 'clinical', and at worst dirty, noisy and with little guarantee of privacy. For some men, one 'failure', or erectile difficulty, begins a vicious circle of fear of failure, leading to anxiety leading to further 'failures'. Together with the probability that not only the clinic, but also his partner is expecting him to 'perform' at the right time, it becomes clear that erectile difficulties are probably common enough for the counsellor to be aware of the likelihood and to check couples' sexual behaviour and satisfaction.

Sometimes couples are asked to have sexual intercourse at a particular time and then to report to the clinic shortly afterwards, so that a post-coital test may be done. The 'pressure to perform' may affect the man's erectile or ejaculatory ability adversely. The woman may develop difficulties in her ability to lubricate vaginally, or to have orgasms, or both. This can make intercourse painful and unsatisfactory for either partner or for both in the couple. They may feel embarrassed by having to attend the clinic flushed, as it were, by their recent sexual activity, when the clinic staff they see will be well aware of the fact that they have had intercourse within the last hour. For many people this is clearly a 'turn off', and leads to anger and resentment between them and possibly also towards the staff. There is also distress that what used to be a private activity is now under third party scrutiny, and this can lead to embarrassment and a sense of shame, adding to that already experienced as a result of the fertility problem.

Many couples go through a period of trying to have sex at the 'right' time of the month. The need of the couple and of the clinic staff to know when ovulation takes place is understandable. However, the attempt to time intercourse to give the sperm and the egg the best chance to meet and to fertilise can be detrimental to the couple's sexual life together. Some individuals feel that their spouse or partner only seems to desire them when there is a chance of conception, and sexual activity can then become a battle-ground for issues of power and control. This is frequently manifested by such statements as 'I don't feel she/he wants me for me, only for the egg/sperm that I have'. There have been cases where a person has woken their spouse in the night with a demand for sexual intercourse because the timing is right in terms of ovulation prediction. In such circumstances with 'performance' being the need and the demand, rather than closeness, affection or lust, it is not surprising that feelings of guilt, shame and anger arise. There are, therefore, battles for control in a situation that feels out of control, about who can 'prove' that they want a child most, about whether a person is lovable enough with or without their fertility.

The counsellor in a fertility unit has an opportunity to dispel myths about sex and reproduction, and to give the appropriate information, as shown in the following example.

Case example

James and Mandy had been referred for sex therapy where the presenting difficulty was one of lack of ejaculatory control that was severe enough for James to be unable, except rarely, to enter the vagina in time before he ejaculated. There was therefore little opportunity for the sperm and the egg to meet and for fertilis-ation to take place. In this case Mandy was very angry about the lack of pregnancy this had apparently caused. James did not seem too concerned, and was less driven to have children in this relationship. After some time it became clear that there was a great deal of pressure on him to 'last a long time' intra-vaginally, and to ejaculate into her vagina, since Mandy had the belief that the chances of conception depended on her having an orgasm, and with penile thrusting alone. This understanding of the perpetuating factor involved in the sexual difficulty made the work easier and much beneficial educative work was done with this couple.

Sexual problems that result in infertility

Sexual problems may result in a lack of conception, prompting a couple to present at an infertility clinic. It is thus important to be clear at the point of assessment what is really happening in this couple's sexual life. 'Infertility examinations should include an evaluation of the sexual behaviour of couples, with special reference to frequency and timing of coitus' (Rantala and Koskimies, 1988: 26). This is important since it may save the couple many months or even years of sitting on waiting lists or having investigations or treatment that may be unnecessary and which may 'embed' the sexual difficulty further, making it less amenable to treatment and causing more distress.

Any of the sexual dysfunctions mentioned earlier may account for the lack of pregnancy, and added to these are two further categories that need to be borne in mind. The first is retrograde ejaculation, where, at orgasm, the ejaculate is expelled back into the bladder rather than through the urethra and thus externally. This can be checked fairly simply by looking at a post-ejaculatory urine sample and seeing if there are sperm to be found in it. The man will experience what is known as a 'dry orgasm', feeling the sensation of ejaculation and orgasm but not producing an ejaculate. Many counsellors will be familiar with this since it is a fairly common presentation in fertility units and can be medically managed, usually fairly successfully. It is, however, important to be aware of the possibility that the man and his partner may have feelings of discomfort or distress about this, and additional areas of sexual difficulty, such as loss of libido or erection problems, may consequently have developed.

The second area that should be considered is whether the sexual activity in which the couple engages is of the kind that may result in pregnancy, that is, that the sperm are being introduced into the vagina. This can mean talking again in very clear terms about the nature of the sexual activity, and not being satisfied with a response such as 'Oh yes, we do it twice a week'. What exactly is it that they 'do' twice a week? Some couples engage in anal intercourse, in umbilical sex, or have manual stimulation alone and are unaware that there is anything else, and so consider that their sexual behaviour is 'normal' and should be resulting in pregnancy.

Thus, there are two main points where the counsellor may be involved. The first is at the point of assessment when the nature of the couple's sexual behaviour needs to be examined carefully and sensitively, and the second is during the investigation and management of the infertility problem, where sexual problems may develop and cause greater distress for the couple in treatment.

Referral issues

As a result of the couple's sexual problems the counsellor may consider that it is appropriate to suggest that the couple accept a referral for psychosexual therapy. The issue of referral for psychosexual therapy is an important one and the following questions should be considered. First, is the problem the result of the infertility diagnosis, investigations and management, or is it the cause or partial cause of the infertility? Secondly, what is the motivation of the individual or couple in addressing the sexual difficulties they have? Is their primary need to have a child, and therefore changing their sexual activity is the means to this, or do they wish to change the way they relate to each other sexually, because they want to have a different and more fulfilling sex life? Are they being sent to a psychosexual therapist because the fertility clinic says so, and they are thus being 'good' patients so that the clinic will keep them on the list for treatment? The answers to these questions will help the counsellor to formulate an appropriate response. For example, if the problem is one which has apparently resulted from the stress of investigations and treatment, it may be possible to encourage the couple to take special time *for themselves*, and for each other, which they may have not done for some time. This could include going back to a class they have stopped attending, deciding on an evening a week that they make their own, to go out, or engage in some activity together. In this way, some couples are reminded of their original enjoyments and pleasures, both as individuals and as a couple, before infertility became such a large part of their lives. This re-establishing of their couple status may be enough to allow them to feel their sexual feelings again. If the problems are more deep-seated, distressing, or existed before a fertility problem was diagnosed, then the counsellor, with the couple, must assess priorities. The timing of referral is important, and it is very difficult and usually unhelpful for couples to engage in psychosexual therapy while they are in the midst of fertility treatments. Either the work must be done between treatments, and this means ensuring a sufficient break of a minimum of four to six months, or when the treatment is over, and there is a decision to end, or there is a pregnancy. In the event of a pregnancy, it may be necessary to wait some months after the baby is born before the couple attends for help with the sexual difficulties.

A clear contract for this type of therapeutic work is essential and the partners need to be committed to the goal of improving their sexual interaction. This is very difficult when sex is seen as the way to have a baby, and has been lost as a way of gaining closeness, intimacy and pleasure. The implications of this for the counsellor working in the fertility unit are that she or he will need to form a judgement about when to refer, and what to do if the couple are unwilling to take up the referral.

Case example

The counsellor had worked with Mary and Richard on the impact of their infertility on their lives, and some grief work had been done. The sessions had also been taken up with working on their communication as a couple, so that they could help each other more effectively when the situation became distressing for either of them.

The counsellor in this example demonstrates working with Mary and Richard on their sexual problem, which was defined as a lack of sexual activity caused by general loss of desire on both their parts. They had identified that this was partially to do with their responses to, and feelings about, their fertility problem. Over time, it emerged that they felt that although their sexual life had never been ideal for either of them, the fertility issues had an effect on them that they wished to examine and correct. Richard had been diagnosed as having azoospermia (total absence of any sperm), and for him sexual activity had taken on different meanings, some of which were about trying to prove that this was not the case (this is seen later in the example), and can be identified as forming a denial response (Kubler-Ross, Stage 1). He also needed to feel accepted *despite his infertility*, and therefore sex became significant for him in a new way. Mary had some difficulty in making these adjustments and was becoming distressed, not only about their infertility, but also about their sex life. They felt angry and resentful both about the infertility itself, and with each other about it, with the result that they both suffered from a loss of desire with a consequent drop in sexual activity.

> *Counsellor*: What do you need to talk about regarding sex?
> *Mary*: That's a very good question.
> *Richard*: I'm frustrated, not sexually frustrated, but frustrated about how I approach it and what I'm doing wrong and why I'm doing it wrong.
> *Counsellor*: I want to come back to this sense you have of doing things wrong, but I want to hear from you, Mary, about how you are feeling about this.

Here the counsellor is eliciting both partners' definitions of the problem, rather than choosing to work with the first that is presented. This is an important part of the skills of working with couples, and in this way the counsellor is showing that she does not necessarily accept the definition presented by Richard as being true for both parties. By inviting Mary to share her understanding of the problem from her perspective the counsellor shows the couple that it is possible to hold differing perspectives of the same series of events and that these are both valid. There will be a more in-depth discussion of the dynamics of working with couples in Chapter 8.

> *Mary*: We have had times when things have been *quite* relaxed and good but I don't think they've ever been really good. I'm sure that it doesn't have to be that way. But on our own we don't seem to have managed to work it out, and more recently we were OK until a few months ago and then we started only having sex on the fertile day. Now we've drifted into really not having sex at all, even then, and I think there's quite a lot of anger about that.
>
> *Counsellor*: You seem angry about this, is that right?
>
> *Mary*: Yes, yes I am.
>
> *Counsellor*: So you Richard are frustrated, and you Mary are angry. What is it that you would like to be different?

The counsellor has moved from defining the problem (using the skills of Egan's Stage 1) to goal setting (Egan, Stage 2).

> *Mary*: I really don't know what the problems are but I know that a little way back, we got into a sort of game where if I asked Richard he'd say no, so when Richard asked me I'd say no. I don't really feel we're in that now which I think is a step forward despite the fact that we're actually having less sex, in fact, none at the moment. We did get quite a long way. I mean we neither of us have a problem with masturbation and things like that and I think there might be a problem around penetrative sex still, in as much as I think Richard's beginning to realise that we don't have to do it and we can still enjoy ourselves. Although there is still a thing about that somewhere, about acceptance probably.
>
> *Counsellor*: Will you say more about what you mean by acceptance?

Here the counsellor is seeking clarification from Mary. It is possible Mary may mean that she thinks Richard wants her to accept him in a sexual way, as a sexual person, or that she believes he wants her to accept him in spite of his infertility. It is important that Mary is asked about this, so she can begin to verbalise her perceptions about the problem. Richard then has the information about how she perceives things between them. The counsellor needs to encourage Mary to be as explicit as possible so that there is as little chance as possible of confusion remaining, which may cause distress and misunderstanding later on.

> *Mary*: I feel that Richard might not feel fully accepted unless we have penetrative sex, and that that is the only proper sort of sex, and I still feel he feels that a bit but I don't know, I could be wrong.
>
> *Richard*: I still feel attracted to Mary.
>
> *Counsellor*: Yes.
>
> *Richard*: If I think we're in danger of having sex then, I stop feeling like it.
>
> *Counsellor*: What is that about for you, do you think?

Richard: I'm not sure, I think I am frightened in case Mary gets angry with me. She has been angry that I want to have sex and that what I want is penetrative sex. It's a case of me getting it wrong again.

Counsellor: So this is part of the issue we have talked of before that has to do with you, Richard, feeling that you have to get everything right and being scared that you might not and at the same time you, Mary, feeling angry that Richard is looking to you to tell him that he is all right, instead of being prepared to take a risk with you. And this is what happens with you when you want to have sex together too, is that right?

Richard: Yes, I guess so.

Here the counsellor is *summarising* the session so far, so all three participants are clear, and also so that the couple may be allowed to feel that they have individually been understood by the counsellor.

At this point the counsellor is making connections with previous work that has been done by this couple in terms of their communication together and linking it to their sexual interaction, thus indicating that sex is not something that is dealt with in isolation.

Counsellor: (*addressing both partners*) Do you feel desire at all?

Mary: Well, my desire disappeared almost totally, although I still enjoy Richard's company particularly when he's not expecting me to mother him a lot of the time. It disappeared with that but it is coming back now really, and I would enjoy all the physical closeness again. I feel that there is something I don't understand preventing Richard and I going any further than we are.

Counsellor: Then you started to have sex on the fertile time. How was that negotiated between you?

Mary: I don't really remember. The point was that it came to being only that somehow, and then when I refused, when I said I didn't want to have sex, Richard got extremely angry and pretty childish.

Richard: I know it was like that sometimes.

Mary: It was related to somehow giving Richard the best chance to have a child.

Richard: It seemed a good idea at the time.

Counsellor: What was that sex like? Was it enjoyable, fun or a bit functional?

Mary: It varied. Trying to get the job done mostly.

Richard: It was variable.

Counsellor: A bit variable.

Richard: Because the timing was fixed, it was . . . From my point of view it was one of the times that I didn't feel particularly keen to have sex.

Mary: And, I think there's, for me, something about the fact that it more or less had to be penetrative sex, it wasn't to do with having sex for fun. A lot of this is around the fun issue again I think.

Here the couple are identifying that sex for fun, as a way of feeling close and intimate, had disappeared. For Richard, who was having some difficulty in accepting his infertility, sexual intercourse had become bound up with an attempt to deny his infertility. It is possible to consider that his need for sex was akin to the 'calling weeping' Leick and Davidsen-Nielsen (1991) describe, and which was discussed in Chapter 5. Richard's difficulties were not helped by drug treatments and surgical intervention, both done in an attempt to improve his sperm count. Hopes were raised that it would be possible to have a biological child of his own and it became impossible for Richard to accept his infertility until much later. His sexual desires became entangled with his need to be accepted totally by his partner, and this was fuelled by a deep fear that she would find him inadequate and leave him. From her viewpoint, his need for her to 'mother' him, by accepting him completely and never allowing any hint of criticism or disappointment in their relationship to surface, was by turns infuriating and distressing. She wanted him to want her, to be interested in her sexually, and to separate his sexual needs from their joint infertility. It was also very important for her to feel that he did see this as a joint problem. She desperately wanted him to acknowledge that while apparently the physical problem was his, there was a loss also for her, in that she would never have *his* child. She also felt resentful that she would have to have investigations and treatments to try to have a child when there was no physical infertility in her that had been identified. Whenever she expressed this resentment, Richard would become defensive and express his needs competitively and in a childlike way that only served to exacerbate her anger.

Their sexual problems had not been caused by their infertility, and indeed they both expressed the opinion that after the diagnosis, initially their sex life and the way they felt about each other had improved.

Counsellor: How have things changed as a result of the fertility problem?
Mary: I feel that things actually got better for a long time, sexually, and in every way.
Richard: We actually got to a better level for a while.
Mary: Yes. We became almost intimate at one point didn't we?
Counsellor: What do you mean by almost intimate?
Mary: I felt that there was communication going on rather than just close your eyes and do it. I mean it was never actually close your eyes and do it but it felt that way. I felt Richard was very impersonal about the way he went about the whole thing. Even though he has always been willing to listen to what I want in a very

practical sense, there was no connection there really. Only occasionally. A lot of the time I felt it was an act of aggression more than of love.

Counsellor: So at what point did you begin to feel that it had become possible to be intimate and communicative and OK together?

Mary: I'm sure we were communicating better generally in our ordinary life, you know it was definitely related to other things apart from sex. It isn't separate from everything else. I think it was probably related to the general level of trust improving.

Richard: It was in between the denial and the grief that things got better.

Counsellor: Tell me what that was like for you, Richard.

At this point, both partners are talking to the counsellor and not to each other. The counsellor needs to take control of this and does so by asking one of them to continue. Alternatively, she could have asked them to talk instead to each other directly. Chapter 8 will explore such strategies in more detail.

Once this initial closeness, which Richard defines as having occurred between the denial and grief stages, changed, there was a growing sense of distance. The most effective way in which Richard felt he could close this was to become very needy. In the beginning Mary tried to meet these needs, but gradually she became increasingly angry that this was how he was behaving and frightened that he was never going to be available for her when she felt needy. As a result the sexual side of their relationship collapsed. This was not really surprising since they were interacting in a 'parent–child' way, and there are strong taboos in our culture about the nature of sexual activity between parents and children (personal communication, R. Little, 1991). Thus if a couple operate in this mode at an emotional and psychological level, sexual activity suffers the force of the taboo. Most couples incorporate elements of nurturing and need for nurture in their sexual lives, which may be seen as 'parent–child' interactions. However, the balance is none the less maintained between these and other appropriate adult responses, which two people need to have for a reasonably happy and functioning sexual life together.

One of the main diagnostic and assessment problems facing a counsellor when working with any sexual problems which arise during infertility treatments or investigations is establishing motivation for change. Do the couple really want to develop or rediscover sexual intimacy together or are they wanting to establish that they are appropriate candidates for parenthood? Or perhaps to give themselves a better chance of conception? Mary and Richard were getting to the stage of wanting to improve their sexual interactions, to allow more intimacy and fun into their lives. They were seeing that there could be advantages for themselves as a couple, whether or not children became part of their lives.

> *Mary*:   Things went quite well when we first got married, when we were presumably trying to have a family without perhaps admitting that to ourselves or each other very openly. I think things went quite well for a short time didn't they, and then it transpired that we had a problem.
>
> *Counsellor*:   How do you think that since then the events of the last 15 months or so, have affected you both sexually?
>
> *Richard*:   They have certainly affected me in the sense that there was a time when I wanted to have sex on fertile days because I thought there was a chance of having a child or having my child and I was indeed very angry when we didn't succeed in having sex on those days. I think I've got to a point now where I don't believe it is likely to produce a child, so from that point of view that specific anger has faded, but sex to me is about duty and responsibility and doing things right. When things were working right or we both felt things were going better I was actually getting to the point when I found some enjoyment in it and it was worth doing in its own right. I believe now that it's worth doing in its own right but I don't seem to be able to get to do it, and so I don't. I'm very wary of it as a subject because it seems to arouse a lot of emotion in me or in Mary, and some of that is negative emotion.
>
> *Counsellor*:   So you say that, historically, sex has been about duty and responsibility and doing it right, and that still now it seems dangerous or difficult for you?
>
> *Richard*:   Yes that's the way it has always been for me.
>
> *Counsellor*:   And now you are seeing that there are important things to be gained from developing a good sexual life with Mary?
>
> *Richard*:   Yes, I think so.

Mary was clearly needing to feel that Richard was interested in her for herself as well as a potential mother for a child they would care for together. It became clear that these issues had echoes for Richard in his childhood experiences of being parented which had had a negative impact on his own sense of self worth and acceptability. Mary began then to feel able to acknowledge that she too had other agendas, as well as wanting to improve her sexual life.

> *Mary*:   I want to consolidate the relationship prior to starting a family and that includes how we are sexually. If we can get it better, that will help us to feel stronger and better parents and that is a healthy thing.

For Richard it seemed that his main anxiety had to do with losing Mary. His self esteem was low for many reasons, most of which had their roots in distressing childhood experiences. There were negative messages for him about sex and sexual behaviour, and a fear of aggression, with a corresponding need to be accepted and loved. When he was diagnosed as being azoospermic, his sense of himself as a man was profoundly shaken and it became very important for him that Mary did not reject him in any way. Any statement or behaviour by her that showed any anger or disappointment was interpreted by him as rejection. One of the results of this was that Mary began to feel unsupported and smothered. She found it difficult to express her own distress and anger at the situation in which they had found themselves, because when she did so, Richard became distressed and guilty. Mary did not find this helpful, and while wanting to support him in his distress also, was unable to find a way of expressing her own needs in a manner that meant that Richard did not become defensive, and was able to support her appropriately.

This took some time for them to recognise, and inevitably the sexual side of their relationship suffered. Much of Richard's motivation to improve their sexual life together came from this fear of rejection, and it was therefore important to clarify his motivation for improving their sexual interaction.

It is perhaps obvious to say that not all couples who need to attend a clinic for infertility investigations or treatment have or develop any sexual difficulties. Indeed, occasionally the process of attending such a unit and having to undergo various forms of examination as well as engaging in explicit discussion of sexual activity and the processes of reproduction, may be therapeutic and may even prevent the development of long-term problems.

The counsellor here is working with a complex mix of issues. These include the impact of the couple's infertility on them as sexual beings, their beliefs about sex and sexual behaviour, their perceptions of themselves as male and female, the roles that they have taken with each other and their beliefs about what they 'should' be like as a couple who wish to be parents. It is necessary to work flexibly with these issues, and be prepared to abandon particular parts of the work at times when the distress of their situation, including their realisation that they have lost sometimes months or years of sexual intimacy and closeness, may need further attention.

8

Counselling Couples

This chapter will explore the dynamics involved in working with couples within the context of fertility issues. First, gender-specific responses to the stress of infertility will be highlighted and discussed. How these stresses are manifested will then be shown by case examples. The second section will examine particular strategies and skills that may be helpful in counselling couples.

Gender issues in the management of infertile couples

There are a number of problems which face the counsellor working in a fertility unit when it comes to counselling couples. First, while medical technology is making advances in the treatment of male infertility, it is still largely the case that the focus of attention is on the woman. This means that apart from early investigations and perhaps some participation in later treatments (the provision of semen samples for example), the male partner is not necessarily involved directly with the procedures. Consequently he may feel excluded, and may have to assert himself, both with the medical staff and with his partner, to ensure that he is included in decision-making about treatments. Any exclusion may reinforce a desire to withdraw or isolate himself from the process that his female partner is, perforce, more actively engaged in.

Secondly, it seems that men and women have, in general, rather different responses to the experience of infertility. This seems to reflect general gender differences in the way in which women and men cope with stressful situations.

> Research suggests that many men only openly express their feelings and concern with their wives, while women have a number of confidants, including their husbands (Cleary and Mechanic, 1983; Khan and Antonucci, 1980). These couples show a similar pattern and this suggests that infertile women experience an extra burden because of their need to provide virtually all of their husbands' social support. (Abbey et al., 1991: 81)

So the *ways* in which the individuals in a couple manage stressful or painful situations are likely to be different and to some extent defined by gender. The likelihood is that women will be going through fertility treatments with all that that entails, as well as supporting their partners. This can lead to feelings of resentment and perhaps anxiety. The woman may feel resentful that she is undergoing medical procedures that are physically invasive, as well as intruding into her time and generally disrupting her life. She may be anxious that if she is providing the support for him, will he be able to support her when she needs it?

In the example of Mary and Richard in Chapter 7, one of Mary's main complaints was that Richard seemed unable to gain support from anywhere else. He did not talk to his friends about his infertility and relied on Mary to supply his emotional support. Mary, while understanding Richard's sadness and occasional despair about his inability to father a child, found that she was becoming increasingly frustrated and angry that when she wanted him to listen to *her* fears and distress about treatments he seemed unable to do so. She also felt physically and emotionally invaded by, and uncomfortable about, the treatments and resented them at times. When Richard was unable to cope with her anger and distress, this increased Mary's sense of isolation.

The counsellor may come across a difference between the partners in the way they understand what support means. This is both culturally and gender defined and there will be exceptions and differences that the counsellor must work to clarify. Typically, however, many men view being supportive as 'being strong' for their partner, and this means that they do not show their own pain and distress. Women often complain that they do not feel supported by this and want their partners to share what they are feeling. This sharing helps them to feel that they are not alone in the experience. As quoted in Stanton's work on 'Cognitive Appraisals, Coping Processes and Adjustment', Mahlstedt (1985) suggested that

> Men, for example, often cope with their pain by keeping it to them-selves and focusing on their wives. Women often cope by talking continually about their pain to their husbands, who, feeling powerless to take away the pain, sometimes stop listening. In order to get him involved, she escalates her complaints and he, in response, retreats even further and may even cease participating in the treatment process. In these cases, the woman feels abandoned when she needs her husband most, and he feels overwhelmed because she needs him so much. (Stanton, 1991: 91)

The following example shows how the different responses to infertility raise the issue of support and how it is manifested within the couple relationship.

Case example

Charlie and Deborah had been together for seven years. They had decided to have a child about three years after they had met. One year later, when Deborah had not as yet conceived, they embarked on a series of investigations which failed to find a definite cause for their problem. Their infertility persisted and they chose to have IVF treatment. Two attempts had not resulted in any pregnancy and they were considering a third try.

During this time Deborah had felt responsible for their childlessness and was tearful and distressed. Initially, Charlie had been sympathetic and reassuring, but as time had gone on, and Deborah's distress each time her period came was no less, Charlie began to withdraw further and further. He spent more time at work, and with his friends from his sporting activities. When they were together he would be unwilling to discuss anything and would barely respond. Although she used a strong support network of friends, her anger towards Charlie grew, and she became depressed and withdrawn.

In this example, Charlie has responded to the stress of the situation in which they as a couple find themselves, by 'stonewalling'. This phenomenon was conceptualised by John Gottman (1991) in a study conducted using couple interaction to predict the longitudinal course of marriages. Stonewalling occurs when a person (usually the man) withdraws as a listener. Gottman describes it in the following manner:

> Stonewalling is a behaviour pattern in which the listener presents a stone wall to the speaker, not moving the face very much, avoiding eye contact . . . holding the neck rigid and not using the usual listener responses such as head nods or brief vocalisations that tell the speaker that the listener is tracking. (1991: 4)

Initially, Deborah responds to this by trying to get Charlie to talk to her. After a time however, when Charlie continues to 'stonewall', Deborah in turn withdraws. This couple relationship is in trouble, and will need help to turn the situation around. Any sharing of feelings needs to be a roughly equal two-way process with each partner 'taking turns' in being the listener, so that the other may express their feelings of loss and anger in the knowledge that these *are* shared by the other.

Quoting Mahlstedt (1985), Abbey, Andrews and Halman say that they

> found that [Mahlstedt's] male infertile clients were not willing to express their fears as openly as were the female clients. This left the wives upset because they felt their husbands were not adequately concerned . . . The general literature on gender difference suggests that women may be more expressive than men (Spence, Deaux and Helmreich, 1985); thus findings for infertile couples reflect general gender differences in the ways in which men and women have been socialised to cope with negative affect. (Abbey et al., 1991: 68–9)

It seems to be the case that the experience of most couples is that the man tries to be the 'strong' one, feeling unable or unwilling to acknowledge his own confusion and pain, concentrating on managing and organising the process in pragmatic ways, or by effectively withdrawing and leaving it to his partner. He may do this in the belief that the fertility problem is more hurtful and damaging for her than for him. Many men are confused and unsure when they are faced with infertility. They enter a world with which their female partners are more likely to be familiar, that is, the world of doctors, gynaecology and investigations, internal examinations and blood samples.

As Marie-Claire Mason, in her book *Male Infertility – Men Talking*, observes:

> Men may feel peculiarly uncomfortable during the investigation phase. They have an uncertain role to play and can feel aimless, useless and unwanted. Guilt and inadequacy can surface because men feel they have inflicted suffering on their partners. These feelings coupled with a sense of powerlessness can make for a disturbing experience which men are unsure how to cope with. (1993: 62–3)

How women and men cope with the experience may be partly culturally, and thus gender, defined. Typically, women value interdependence and similarity, and men value autonomy and independence. Women may feel hurt and unhappy that their partners are unable to share their feelings about what is happening to them. Men may be confused and unsure about what to do to help. What the nature of support should be may be very different. Stereotypically for women it may be talking it through many, many times. For men it may be trying to forget about it, spending time with those who are *not* going to talk about it, or in activities such as work or sport. Both women and men will, at times, want to talk about it, and not talk about it, and to bury themselves in other things. Problems occur both for the individuals within the couple and for the couple relationship when the status quo is disturbed and the coping mechanisms that each uses are in conflict. 'Both males and females who coped through avoidance evidenced more distress. In addition, males who use confrontive and self controlling coping were more distressed, as were females who accepted responsibility for their infertility problem' (Stanton, 1991: 97).

Strategies for use in counselling couples

As discussed in Chapter 2, couples and individuals may respond to a diagnosis or realisation that they have a fertility problem with disbelief. They may deny the existence of the problem, or they may minimise the significance of the problem. Not only may they withdraw from family and friends, but they may also withdraw and isolate themselves from their partner or spouse (Kubler-Ross's Stage 1).

Case example

The following example shows how the first stage that Kubler-Ross describes, Denial and Isolation, may contribute to the stress that couples experience as a result of a fertility problem. The counsellor's task here is to facilitate the re-establishment of communication between the couple.

David had recently been diagnosed as being azoospermic. His wife, Penny, had been devastated about this, since she had married David especially to have children. (They had been living together for some time before their marriage.) Penny had had two terminations of pregnancy, two and five years before she and David had met. David had responded stoically to the diagnosis that he had no sperm. He had told Penny that it didn't matter, that he felt fine about it, and that they would look at other ways to have a family. Significantly, he had not told anyone else about their fertility problem, and had asked Penny not to say anything either. Penny was very distressed and angry, and felt that she had no one with whom she could discuss her feelings.

They attended counselling together on the suggestion of their family doctor, after Penny had visited her, and had told her that she thought the relationship was 'over'.

> *Counsellor*: Will you tell me what you would like to gain from this time today?

Here, the counsellor is getting a *contract* for the session. I have found, in my work with couples, that this process of contracting is very useful for three main reasons. First, it clarifies the goals that each of the couple have, and secondly, as a result of that, provides helpful material and insight into the differences and similarities that the couple have. Thirdly, the couple may not have known that they have these differences and similarities, and this acknowledgement during the contracting process alone may prove useful as well as therapeutic.

> *Penny*: Well, our doctor sent us. We found out six months ago that we wouldn't be able to have any children of our own, and since then we haven't got on very well together. David never talks to me, and I feel so lonely. He won't let me tell anyone and I really need to talk to someone about it all.

The counsellor is being appealed to by Penny, and she could in response to this appeal ask her to talk directly to David (the skill of *decentering*, discussed later in this chapter). However, as this is very early in the session and there is no agreement between them and the counsellor yet as to what they wish to gain from the session, that is to say there is no contract for the session, the counsellor chooses to move directly on to David and asks him what his needs are in the counselling session.

> *Counsellor*: So, Penny, you want to talk about what these past few months since you found there is a fertility problem have been like for you. David, will you tell me what it is that you want from this session?
> *David*: I don't know really. Penny is very upset about this, and it is true that we haven't been getting along very well lately, but I don't know what she wants from me. It's not as if we can change anything. Talking about this is not going to make me fertile, is it? What Penny wants is a baby, and I can't give her a baby can I? What is there to say?
> *Penny*: That's what he does all the time now, it's as though he's behind a wall. I can't reach him. It makes me furious.

It is clear that David has withdrawn and isolated himself from Penny, who seems to be feeling increasingly angry and distressed by this. However, the more she attempts to get him to respond to her, the more David withdraws. Penny is becoming evermore tearful and volatile and David is becoming more and more stoical, logical and 'rational'. The divide between them is growing wider.

Figure 8.1   *The counsellor facing a mutually withdrawn couple*

For many this withdrawal may be a response to the experience of pain. There may also be an unrealistic hope that if they do not discuss or acknowledge what is happening, the problem will go away, or will not hurt so much. The infertile person may say, 'Well, I don't like to talk about it, it only upsets me, and then she/he gets emotional too, that doesn't help to solve the problem, does it?' The other partner in the relationship often experiences this withdrawal, this refusal to discuss what is happening to them, as painful and confusing. Many respond by becoming angry, and withdraw in their turn. Thus, a counsellor may be faced with a couple who are distanced from one another, angry, confused and lonely within this relationship. Figure 8.1 gives an idea of how this may look.

Working with couple problems

An important task for the counsellor is to facilitate communication between the individuals within the couple relationship. In Figure 8.1 the counsellor is placed, metaphorically and dynamically, outside but, at the same time, between the couple. The individuals in such a couple will often address what they have to say to the counsellor, and not to each other. This may be the case particularly in couples where anger and conflict are close to the surface. Each member of the couple may look to the counsellor to act as a judge for them, to tell them which one is right or wrong, good or bad, reasonable or unreasonable. One of the skills that a counsellor may use in working with this dynamic is decentering (Crowe and Ridley, 1990: 95–7). This is where the counsellor resists any attempt to be drawn in as judge or advocate for one partner or the other, and encourages the comments and questions each puts to the other.

Case example

Returning to the example of Penny and David discussed earlier, it was apparent within the first few minutes of the counselling session that each was distanced from the other. Having understood that what Penny wanted from the counselling was to have David communicate with her, and for her hurt and distress to be heard, it was also clear that the dynamic was that if the counsellor 'pursued' David further to express his feelings, he would respond in the way he had done with Penny over the previous six months, that is, by withdrawing. The counsellor opts instead to help Penny and David unravel their communication, in the following manner:

> *Counsellor*: You say, David, that there is nothing to say about this and that talking about it won't change the fact that you are infertile. That's true, talking won't change it.

The counsellor is acknowledging the reality of David's infertility, and in so doing begins the process of helping *him* to face it (Worden's Task 1). Here David looks a little surprised, but offers no comment. The counsellor continues as follows:

> *Counsellor*: Perhaps it might be useful to look at what has happened to your relationship together since you got the news of your infertility, since it seems that things have changed as a result of it. Would you be willing to do that?

The counsellor is again getting an agreement, or a contract, about the work to be done.

> *David*: Well, I suppose so, but I think it's Penny who needs the help really. She's so upset about it, and I don't know what to do.

The counsellor could engage in a dialogue with David at this point, but chooses to use decentering skills to work towards the goal of clearer communication.

> *Counsellor*: Will you face Penny, look at her and tell *her* that?
> *David*: [*looking uncomfortable and slightly embarrassed*] Well, she knows, what's the point?
> *Penny*: [*to the counsellor*] This is just what he does all the time, it's so frustrating, can't you get him to talk about it more?
> *Counsellor*: [*refusing to be drawn into taking one side or the other, and addressing them both*] What I notice is that you both seem to believe that the other has the more important or painful problem, and that it appears that you are trying to care for each other in this way.

Here, the counsellor is communicating empathic understanding by using summary and paraphrasing. This is an Egan Stage 1 skill. The counsellor continues:

Counsellor: Penny, you said just now that 'that's what he always does'. Will you face David, turn your chair towards his, and tell him what it is that he 'always does'?

Penny: [*Having shifted her seat and facing David*] You close off, just when I think you are going to say how you feel, you stop, you tell me I'm upset, but a lot of that now is because you won't let me in. You sound so low and flat, I can see that you are sad too, but you won't let me help . . .

David: [*starting to reply*] I don't know what . . .

Counsellor: [*interrupting*] David, will you wait a moment. Penny, when you experience David as 'closing off', what is that like for you, how do you feel?

The counsellor has interrupted David here because it is important that the couple do not just go straight into the whole round of discussion that they have already demonstrated at the beginning of the session, and which they are very familiar with. They need to have a different experience of communication, and part of that is becoming more aware of what it is that they individually are feeling and how the other person affects them, as well as what they would like the other to do differently.

Penny: It feels horrible.

Counsellor: Will you tell David that you feel horrible when he does that.

Penny: I feel horrible when you do that. I feel as though I'm worthless and useless. [*Begins to cry.*]

David: I don't know what you want from me. I can't give you a child . . . [*Here David stops and looks at the counsellor as if for help.*]

The counsellor chooses to continue with the work of facilitating the communication between them, rather than challenge David's apparent lack of empathy and passive request for help.

Counsellor: How do you feel that you can't give Penny a child. Tell Penny.

David: I feel awful. I wonder why you stay with me. I know that you married me because you wanted children and now we can't have them we might as well get divorced.

It is becoming clearer in the session that David is fearful of losing Penny, and by denying the significance of the problem, and withdrawing from Penny, is perhaps hoping to avoid painful discussions where the issue of Penny leaving him (to have children with another man?) is raised. By encouraging him to speak directly to Penny, the counsellor has facilitated David in beginning to tell Penny of his fears of losing her and of his sense of worthlessness. This, in turn, allows Penny to feel less excluded, and Penny is able to let David know that she is feeling useless within the relationship.

By supporting direct communication, and the use of 'I' statements, as shown in this example, the counsellor is able to help the couple towards the goal of clear communication. This will then allow them to make clearer and better decisions about their life together. In this way the counsellor avoids the trap of adjudicating the behaviour of two squabbling children and helps them to manage the conflict between them.

Confronting self-defeating communication

A further strategy that may help the counsellor to facilitate communication between the couple is to work with them through the ways in which they do communicate. It is useful here to have a concrete experience that the couple bring to the session, or to use one that occurs within the session itself. Many individuals in a couple relationship complain that the other 'doesn't really listen', that 'nothing ever changes' as a result of an argument. The arguments are always the same, they go around the same old circuit and end in the same familiar way with them both feeling more isolated and misunderstood than ever.

A couple may show the counsellor, in the session, what happens when they argue. It is useful for the counsellor to stop this in mid flow, and to ask the couple the following questions.

Useful questions for the counsellor

- How are you feeling now? [to each partner]
- What will happen next?
- What do you want now instead of what is happening?
- Are you getting what you want?
- Do you expect to get what you want now?
- If this goes on how will it end?

Based on a workshop presentation by R. Little, 1991

In being challenged to consider these questions the couple may become aware that they are in fact, in arguing, attempting to get some result, which they may be unaware of. They may also see that this way of trying to get this need met is not effective, and that there is little evidence that it will be effective. This may be a revelation to them. However, it is often very difficult for couples to stop arguing, since while they may realise that this is not going to produce the result that they want, which is usually a feeling that they are understood and feel close to the other (that is, intimacy), they are paradoxically intensely engaged with one another during the argument. This is not a comfortable or loving engagement, but it is, none the less, engrossing and deeply felt. It is therefore difficult for couples to surrender this way of attempting to communicate, despite the pain they both experience.

Case example

The case of Robin and Lesley illustrates well the way in which this dynamic operates. This couple had been married for 15 years, and for 10 years had been actively pursuing, in one way or another, the goal of having children, including several years of fertility treatments. They were referred for counselling when at Lesley's fifth IVF attempt she had disclosed to a member of staff that she had been upset to discover that Robin had been involved since the previous year in a relationship with another woman.

The counsellor had seen them several times and it was clear that Robin had found the strain of supporting Lesley through the fertility treatments, as well as dealing with his own feelings about their lack of children, very hard to bear. As a result he had felt vulnerable enough to begin a relationship with someone else; a relationship in which the woman was not making these demands on him, and in which he experienced fun and laughter, something that had been missing for him in the recent years of his marriage with Lesley. Lesley perceived this 'affair' as a betrayal of the deepest kind. She was devastated by it, and it added to the sense of loss and despair she felt as a result of her childless state. They seemed unable to hear each others' viewpoint, and were living at high level of tension which was rapidly becoming insupportable.

The counsellor's work in the following example is first to help them to see how their attempts at communicating with each other do not result in a sense of being understood by the other, or in agreement or useful negotiation, and secondly to begin the task of helping them to communicate more effectively.

Lesley begins the session immediately they sit down, and attacks Robin for his faithlessness.

> *Lesley*: You have betrayed me in the worst possible way, just when I needed you most. I can't believe you would do that. If there was one thing I thought I was sure of it was that you would never be unfaithful. I can never trust you now [*collapsing into tears*], I've lost everything.

Robin: What can I do to convince you that I do care about you? [*Turning to the counsellor*] I don't know what to do, she's being so unreasonable, she's never willing to understand what *I've* gone through.

Lesley: That's not true. I've spent hours comforting you, you wanted children so badly, but I'm the one who has had to go through all the procedures, all so that we could have a family, and then you do this.

Counsellor: [*in a very firm voice*] I want you both to stop this now. [*Pause*] This is a very familiar argument isn't it? If you carry on with it how will you both end up feeling?

Lesley and Robin both look surprised, and after a pause Robin continues:

Robin: Well, I guess Lesley gets more and more angry and upset . . .

Counsellor: Robin, will you say how *you* end up feeling at the end of this kind of fight?

The counsellor does not allow Robin to continue to define what Lesley does, but asks Robin to consider *his* responses, to become aware of his own behaviour.

Robin: Oh. Well, I suppose I get frustrated, I mean, she's so unreasonable.

Counsellor: Robin, will you stay with how *you* feel?

Robin: [*after a pause*] Helpless really. I don't know what to do. It's all such a mess.

The counsellor allows the silence that follows this statement to continue for a while. This is to allow the couple to experience what is happening. The counsellor has been observing Lesley's behaviour, and has noticed that Lesley is quiet and looking a little tearful.

Counsellor: Robin, I'm going to leave you with that for a moment. Lesley, when you have these fights, how do *you* usually feel at the end of them?

Lesley: Very angry, and as though I'm being unreasonable. I feel alone.

Counsellor: So Robin, you feel frustrated and helpless, and Lesley, you feel angry and lonely. When you start off the discussions that turn into argument what do you *want* to say to each other?

Lesley: I want him to know how bad I feel.

Counsellor: And when he knows how bad you feel, how will you know? What would show you that he understands?

Lesley: I don't know . . . I would just know . . . I would feel better.

The counsellor has uncovered the belief Lesley has that, roughly summarised, is, 'If he really cared about me he would know what to do without me having to say or do anything'. This belief may be held by both Lesley and Robin, and many of this couple's difficulties may be maintained by it. They both *think* they are being clear with each other, and therefore when they do not get the response they want, they consider the other does not *care* enough for them to respond in the way that they want.

The counsellor chooses here to challenge this as follows:

Counsellor: What would you like from Robin that would let you know that he understands?
Lesley: I'd like him to stop being so *reasonable*.
Counsellor: [*persisting with this*] Lesley, instead of saying what you *don't* want, will you say what you *do* want from Robin that would help you to know that he understands?
Lesley: I want him to tell me that he's sad about what has happened to us, that he is angry that we can't have children, you've never told me that.
Robin: But you *know* that . . . surely . . .
Lesley: No I don't. You've been really great over the years supporting me, but I've never heard you say how you feel about it, it would help me.

The counsellor has stopped the usual, familiar pattern of the argument, which is an attempt by Lesley and Robin to get the other to meet a need for reassurance and for intimacy. The counsellor has facilitated them, first, to recognise what they are feeling, and secondly, the counsellor has then helped Lesley to formulate what she wants from Robin that may help her to feel that he understands.

The work has moved on from stopping Robin and Lesley communicating in old, self-defeating ways to helping them communicate more usefully. The communication model outlined below is a framework for use when helping couples learn to communicate effectively.

Communication model

This model has been developed from St George's Hospital (London) Training Workshops, forming part of the Diploma and MSc courses in Human Sexuality, 1981–1994.

Phase One of this model of communication can be broken down into the following four steps.

1   *Recognise and name own feelings.* This is often the most difficult part of the process for the couple. Many couples are so involved in *responding* to the other that they do not stop to monitor what they are *feeling*. Note the process that occurred with Robin at the beginning of the case example above. When encouraged to slow down and to consider his own feelings, he was able to say that he felt helpless.

2 *Communicate these to the other*. This is also difficult, but can be practised in the session as shown above. Essentially the counsellor would encourage the couple to state directly what they feel. For example, 'I feel angry/sad/happy (feeling) when you say/do (action)'. This feeling/action statement (Steiner, 1986: 130) allows individuals to say what they feel without attributing blame to the other. It is giving information to their partner about what their response is.

3 *Formulate a desired response from the other*. When the person has made a feeling/action statement, they can then consider what it is that they would like the other to do that would be different. This must be realistic and specific, not punitive or general. The example of Lesley in the above case shows how this operates. Lesley was initially finding it difficult to think of something possible and specific that Robin could *do* that would indicate to her that he cared. With encouragement from the counsellor, Lesley found something that Robin could *do* that would help.

4 *Request this response*. This should preferably be phrased positively. In the example above, Lesley initially phrased what she wanted negatively:

> *Lesley*: I'd like him to stop being so *reasonable*.
> *Counsellor*: [*persisting with this*] Lesley, instead of saying what you *don't* want, will you say what you *do* want from Robin that would help you to know that he understands?

An example of a clear request using the whole of the above process would be something like, 'I feel angry when you don't come to the clinic with me, and what I would like you to do is to arrange to come with me next time.'

Each partner needs to go through these four steps in turn, and then to learn to develop and expand the communication, so that it operates as an interactional process. This is Phase Two of the model and is shown below using the case of Ashok and Rabeena, a couple referred for counselling because of relationship difficulties.

1 *Recognise and name own feelings*
   For example, Ashok is aware of feeling irritated.
2 *Communicate the feelings through an action/feeling statement, to the other*
   For example, 'Rabeena, I was angry when you turned away just now.'

3   *Other acknowledges the feelings expressed*
    For example, 'I understand you are angry with me because I looked away.'
4   *Formulate a desired response, or change in behaviour*
    For example, Ashok is aware that what he wants is for Rabeena to look at him when he talks to her.
5   *Request this*
    For example, 'What I would like you to do instead is to look at me when I talk to you.' *Or*, the other asks, 'Is there something you want from me?'
6   *Acknowledgement of request and agreement to do it*
    For example, 'That's fine, Ashok. I am willing to look at you when you are talking to me.' *Or*
    Re-negotiate
    For example, 'I am willing to look at you when you are talking to me. What I want from you, is that you stop wagging your finger at me whilst you talk. Is that OK with you?' Ashok agrees to the re-negotiated compromise.

As shown above this process of negotiation can continue to a conclusion that is good enough for both parties. The negotiation that is necessary to allow change cannot happen if there has not been an acknowledgement of the feelings involved. In that case, the attempt to negotiate founders at the point of trying to be heard and understood, and the conflict therefore continues.

This process means that a couple will have to slow down the communication with each other, and be prepared to take the time necessary to learn to talk to each other. For couples leading busy lives who are also involved with fertility investigations and treatments, this may mean changing the patterns of their day-to-day lives. Many couples do not expect to make time together a priority. However, this may be one of the most useful things that a counsellor can suggest.

It has been acknowledged that fertility problems cause stress in the individuals within a couple. Men and women appear to manage their stress in different and more or less useful ways. In one study it was shown that stress was experienced by men and women in response to different stimuli, as well as there being an overall joint perception of stress when faced with treatment.

For both women and men, stress was significantly positively correlated with treatment costs and number of tests and treatments received; stress was significantly negatively correlated with confidence that one will have a child and perceived control. For women only, attitudes about infertility treatments, importance of children, attributions of responsibility to physicians, and social support also significantly related to perceived stress. For men only, income, number of physicians seen, and self attributions of responsibility also significantly related to perceived stress. (Abbey et al., 1992: 122)

How this stress operates on the couple relationship clearly affects the health of the relationship as a whole.

The strategies discussed in this chapter to help the counsellor in a fertility unit to work with couples may be sufficient to allow the couple to decrease the levels of stress that exist within their relationship. Along with help in controlling their situation, as discussed in Chapter 3, reduction in stress will help the couple to experience the whole process of fertility treatments more positively. The counsellor should, however, be alert to more intractable difficulties that a couple may be experiencing and make appropriate referral to a relationship counsellor or therapist.

9

Fertility Counselling and Issues of Donation

The use of donated genetic material is not a new phenomenon. Indeed, it is likely that semen from a brother or lover has been used 'unofficially' for millennia to overcome childlessness. 'It is a wise man who knows his father', so the saying goes, and this is borne out by various research programmes looking at different social or genetic areas of interest, in which it has been discovered that there is indeed a high proportion of children who could not be those of the man whom they call 'father'. In his book *The Language of Genes*, Steve Jones states

> Not all families are what they seem. Attempts to match the genes of parents and offspring in Britain or the United States reveal quite a high incidence of false paternity. Many children have a combination of genes which cannot be generated by combining those of their supposed parents. Usually they show that the biological father is not the male who is married to the biological mother. In middle-class society about one birth in twenty is of this kind. (1994: 29–30)

Thus at some cultural level there may be an understanding that semen is 'spread', often widely, in the population with resulting uncertainty over paternity. This may have helped to make donor insemination acceptable in a way that perhaps ovum donation is not as yet. The one certainty that humans had, usually, was who their mother was: someone, somewhere knew, even in cases of adoption, who had given birth to any particular child. In the case of either semen or ova the *conscious* and *overt* decision to use donated genetic material has caused distress and often anger amongst some sections of society.

Donor insemination, involving a medical third party to assist with the procedure was documented in *Medical World* in 1909 and described events which took place in 1884 (Cusine, 1988: 13). This occurred in Philadelphia and the account of it began a heated debate which continues to the present day as to the ethics, morality, safety and wisdom of the use of donated gametes to overcome childlessness. The earliest accounts of the use of donor insemination in the UK date from the late 1930s and this practice became more widespread with the development of cryo-preservation techniques during the late 1940s.

What is a new and, for some, a far more disturbing development, is the use of donated ova, which now means that it is possible to separate the 'genetic' mother from the 'birth' mother. Many feel profoundly uncomfortable about this, and their discomfort is reflected in some of the couples who find themselves with that option as their best or only hope of a child. Some must overcome quite a high level of uncertainty about it before they are able to move forward. Some are unable to do this and so end their quest for a child through any of the assisted conception techniques.

This chapter will consider semen donation and ovum donation, the arguments for and against whether to tell the child of the manner of its conception, and its genetic origins, the impact of the loss of the genetic link, and the issues that surround 'known' donation.

Semen donation

Semen donation is used when the husband's or partner's sperm is absent, present in low numbers, or not of sufficient quality to fertilise an ovum. Most semen donation is done anonymously. One of the issues that does arise with semen donation is whether to use a mixture of the donor's and husband's or partner's semen, so that the couple could never be quite sure whether any pregnancy is as a result of the donor or the husband or partner. This is recommended at times, perhaps in an attempt to help the couple to come to terms with the situation, although it seems to me to be misguided and does not help the couple either to face their fertility problem or to make a clear and adult decision about their options. There is also the question of whether it is in the best interests of the child that there is confusion about its genetic origins. This practice is less common now than it once was, and in general this is a good thing.

Figures for 1992, published in the Human Fertilisation and Embryology Authority's Annual Report for 1994 show that in the UK the main indicator for donor insemination treatment was, unsurprisingly, male sub-fertility or infertility. Pregnancy rates drop significantly with an increasing number of previous attempts, and there is a pregnancy rate of 3.8 per cent per treatment cycle in women who are over 45 years old, and a live birth rate of 1.3 per cent. The overall pregnancy rate in the UK's 85 fertility centres was 6.7 per cent per treatment cycle with a live birth rate of 5 per cent per treatment cycle (HFEA, 1994: 41–2).

Ovum donation

This is a way in which women who are unable to produce any ova, or ova of sufficient quality for fertilisation, may be helped to carry and deliver a child, through the use of donated ova which are then fertilised, using the usual IVF techniques, with the husband's or partner's sperm (donated sperm may also be used).

The main client groups for this technique are women who are peri- or post-menopausal, and this may include women in their 40s–50s, as well as young women in their 20s who have had a premature menopause; or women who have absent ovaries due to previous surgical procedures.

> Since the first pregnancy was reported in 1983 by Trounsen et al. ovum donation has been used in women with genetic disorders, ovarian failure, resistant ovaries and in women who have failed ovulation induction and in-vitro fertilization (IVF) treatments. (Kirkland et al., 1992: 355)

The use of donated ova, as with any of the advances in reproductive technology, brings new and sometimes baffling issues for all concerned to grapple with.

To tell or not to tell?

Many couples have strong opinions about whether or not they will tell the child of its origins. The arguments *against* are based on the notion that the child will be unable to understand what this is all about. Couples already feel very protective of this potential child, and perhaps wish to shield it from knowledge that it may find difficult or painful. Many believe that the child will feel confused and unhappy about the difference in the way it was conceived, that it will be unable to assimilate this information, and that it will be subject to ridicule and stigma from others about the fact that it is 'unusual' in some way.

There are variations on the need for privacy as far as telling other people is concerned. Some infertile men feel strongly that they do not want to deal with the inconsiderate comments of others, who associate fertility with virility and sexual performance, and therefore wish this information to be kept private. Some will want no one at all to know, apart from their wife or partner. Others will want to let the child know in time, but not the family or the wider circle of friends. Women who are in the position of needing to use donated ova often feel that the fact that they will carry and deliver any child conceived as a result means that they are 'the mother' and do not want to complicate things by differentiating between the genetic mother and the birth mother. Some couples feel that the use of donor gametes represents a failure in themselves and therefore do not wish to inform anyone. There has been relatively little experience of this aspect of the 'new' technologies and their impact on families, and further research is needed.

The arguments *for* telling the child are based on the idea that it is very difficult to keep this kind of information from the person most closely involved, that is, the child. It seems that if anyone has been told of the need for the use of donated gametes, such as the parents or siblings of the infertile couple or person, then the child will have to be told in time. A family secret may well be as destructive to the welfare of the child as the information is feared to be. Children seem to be able to sense when there is a secret of this nature and will feel uncomfortable. They are often well able to adapt to the information as long as the parents themselves are clear about their roles and their feelings, and are able to tackle the child's concerns openly and with care. Telling the child avoids the trauma of disclosure at a difficult or sensitive time, such as the separation or divorce of the parents, or through a medical procedure which may uncover the genetic 'mismatch'.

In one British study, '74 per cent of recipients had told at least one person other than their partner about their efforts . . . Approximately half our recipients intend to tell the child, and as the children resulting from oocyte donation are still young, their likely attitude in relation to seeking the donor is not known' (Kirkland et al., 1992: 357)

Potential parents are concerned to do the best that they can for this hoped-for child and the counsellor's task is to help them to explore all the issues and to arrive at some agreement between them as to their preference about telling the child. This is important since any difference of opinion within the couple will show and the child may well become confused and distressed. The difficulty in this task is that the counsellor and couple are discussing what is really a hypothetical question. Some couples find this hard and do not want to consider it until there is a pregnancy. There is perhaps a sense of 'tempting providence' in such discussions. The counsellor must respect the prospective parents' choice, while giving them the relevant information about the latest research, and must lead the couple through the possible consequences of decisions that they make now. An exploration of the way in which they communicate and negotiate desired changes may help the couple to reassure themselves that decisions made now do not have to be 'set in concrete', although there may be consequences for which they must take responsibility.

Useful questions for the counsellor

- Who knows that you have a fertility problem?
- What do they know about it?
- How have they responded?
- If you tell your parents that you are going to have donated sperm/ova, how are they likely to view that?
- How does this impact on whether you tell any child about their origins?
- What concerns do you have about using donor sperm or ova?
- What consideration have you given to the question of telling the child about its conception and origins?

If, in response to the first two questions, 'Who knows that you have a fertility problem?' and 'What do they know about it?', the couple state that everyone in the family knows that, for example, the woman has gone through an early menopause at the age of 25, or that the man has very poor quality sperm, then it is useful to help them to explore what they are considering telling their family and friends about the conception of the child. It is possible that some couples have not thought through the consequences of having told other people and may need room to do so. If no one has been told anything definite about the nature of the fertility problem, then there is sometimes more room to explore options about what to tell people, including any child.

The third question, 'How have they responded?', helps the counsellor to assess what levels of support the couple have in general, and may help the couple to clarify what they wish to say, and to whom. This question is linked to the fourth one, 'If you tell your parents that you are going to have donated sperm/ova, how do you think they are likely to view that?' Often couples are particularly concerned about the parental response to the use of donated gametes. The counsellor may need to help them explore their fears and formulate proactive communication with the parent or parents involved.

The fifth question, 'How does this impact on whether you tell any child about their origins?', helps the counsellor to clarify how much the couple have been looking forward to the possibility of a child or how much they have been going through the process one step at a time, without perhaps daring to project too far into the future. The couple are often in the position of considering hypothetical scenarios, at the same time as wanting to conserve their energies for the task in hand, that is, the next treatment. The seventh question, 'What consideration have you given to the question of telling the child about its conception and origins?', will often also be covered here in this discussion.

The sixth question, 'What concerns do you have about using donor sperm or ova?', helps to clarify what particular issues this couple have about donation. There may perhaps be some difficulty coming from a religious belief, or anxiety about the screening process that the clinics give the donors that they use.

Case example

Mark, who is 27, and his partner Jenny, aged 25, had been told that Mark was azoospermic. This was painful for them, but was also very difficult since they were considering using donor sperm from an anonymous donor and Mark felt strongly that his father would be unable to accept a grandchild 'not of his blood'.

As a couple who wished to do what they considered to be the best for their potential child, they felt they wanted to tell the child of its origins and how it was conceived. They were anxious not to lie to the child or to their parents. However they were fearful that Mark's father would reject the child. They wanted the support of Jenny's parents, who they thought would readily accept any child they had. This meant that either both sets of parents or neither should be told. To do otherwise, they felt, was divisive and risky in terms of potentially damaging disclosure to the child at an inappropriate time.

The counsellor's task here was to help them to weigh up their needs for support against the possible conflict and rejection from Mark's father; their desire to choose *for themselves as a couple* what they felt would be best for this potential child, versus their responsibilities to the wider family. The necessary separation of roles is often the focus of the work here. Mark's needs and expectations as a son to his father (his son role) and his care and responsibility as a father to a child (his father role), needed to be teased out, balanced and weighed, so that he could decide on which to base these significant and far-reaching decisions. As well as this, there was his relationship with Jenny (his partner role), and their joint responsibility to each other, in considering the impact of *their* choices on any child.

The genetic link

Some couples find it hard to face the loss of the genetic link from the past to the future, and will go to great lengths so that their own genetic material can be used. This may seem more significant for them than having *any* child, and some will withdraw from the treatment programme if they are unable to have their own 'biological' child. This decision must be respected, and suitable counselling or therapy offered if needed to manage the grief process.

The notion of 'genetic death', although rare in my experience, is one that some infertile people relate to strongly. It seems to be linked with a deep sense of loss and worthlessness. For those who identify this as relevant to them there is a strong impetus to 'leave something behind' when they die. This 'something' is a child who is linked genetically to them. There is a profound need not to be the last in the line, not to be the one who allowed the family to end. It is as though they cannot bear to take this responsibility, that they feel they are letting down the generations before them, and that if they can leave a biologically linked child behind, then they have done their part in keeping the chain alive. I have noticed that the idea of genetic death seems to be more common in men than in women, although it is in general not common. It is again an area that needs further research.

'Known' donation

One of the things that seems to concern those who are considering using donated gametes, is their fear of feeling invaded by an unknown quantity, not just into their lives as a couple, but also and in a very real sense, into the body of the woman. She will be carrying, and they as a couple will be preparing for, a child half (and sometimes all) of whose genetic material comes from an unknown source. For some, this is deeply uncomfortable and distressing. In an attempt to gain some control in this situation and to relieve their discomfort, as in the case of Rose and Joe described in Chapter 4, couples may wish to use the sperm or eggs of a relative or friend. The knowledge about where the genetic material came from gave this couple a sense of security and safety, which was important to them. For those for whom a genetic link is especially important the preference would clearly be for genetic material from a sister or brother (depending obviously on the need), or perhaps a cousin.

Known donation raises various concerns that focus around the possible difficulty that those involved may have in their relationships with the donor if a pregnancy occurs, or indeed if it does not. These concerns include the possible confusion of roles for those involved in this process; jealousy and envy interfering in family relationships, or in friendships; and special difficulties in adjusting to the situation should there be a child who is abnormal or disabled in some way, or where conception does not take place. I want briefly to look at these areas in turn before going on to present two illustrative case examples.

Confusion of roles
Perhaps more in the case of ovum donation than in semen donation, known donation raises uncomfortable feelings. This is especially so if the donor and recipient are sisters. The fact that it is now possible that a child's 'birth' mother and 'genetic' mother are two different people is difficult enough, but that the 'birth' mother and the 'genetic' mother are sisters, thus making the 'genetic' mother the child's 'social'/'familial' aunt, is even more confusing for many people. Concern has been expressed that the 'mother' and the 'aunt' would be unable to manage these roles satisfactorily with regard to the child. There is a fear that the 'aunt' would inevitably feel as though she were the 'mother', thus causing the 'birth' mother to feel angry and jealous, with consequent effects on the child of confusion and distress. Many, both working in infertility and outside the field, are worried about the potential for family friction and even breakdown as a result. It has, however, been my experience that sister-to-sister donation is in general, carefully thought through. The donor often feels very sad for her sister, and having children herself (as is usually the case), wants to help. Very often she will make statements such as, 'My eggs will only go to waste anyway, it seems so silly not to use them for my sister who has none.'

The recipient is often concerned not to put any pressure on her sister, but does feel that this option suits her best. She will know the origin of the genetic material, it is close to her own, and so erroneously she may think that there is more chance of the treatment working successfully. (There is no evidence that genetically linked donation results in more successful outcomes.) In many cases, all three sets of potential grandparents (that is, the sisters' parents and each of the husband's or partner's parents) know the situation and are supportive. There seems to be a general attitude of acceptance and support in these families . However, there has been no long-term research thus far, specifically looking at families in which known, especially sibling to sibling, donation has happened, and what its effects have been.

As far as semen donation is concerned, the arguments are less heated now, although many people are still uncomfortable with it. Some consider that semen donation amounts to adultery. In a book entitled *Ethics, Reproduction and Genetic Control*, there is the following discussion of this issue, in a chapter entitled 'Marriage and the Family', written by the Board for Social Responsibility: 'AID may be compared to adultery in so far as the presence of the child is founded on a genetic union that is extrinsic to the family.' Some people who hold strong religious views may feel that this is the case. However, the authors go on to say, 'Of course, there is no offence against the married partner, there is no breaking of the relationship of physical fidelity and there is no real relationship with a person outside the marriage. It is certainly quite unlike the physical act of adultery therefore' (Chadwick, 1992: 58).

The counsellor must be aware, when working with those who are considering the use of donated gametes, of the clients' possible distress, confusion and occasionally distaste about such use, and be willing to make such feelings overt as far as possible so that any decision may be made clearly with less unexpressed fear, resentment or anxiety. For those for whom the genetic link is important, using the semen of a brother or cousin is often the preferred option. This does not necessarily have to be done in a clinic setting at all, unless there is a need for specific tests or for cryo-preservation techniques. Self insemination has been used in many cases.

There does seem to be a group of men, as discussed in Chapter 7, whose sense of sexual adequacy is linked to their ability to produce 'good' sperm. The use of a brother's sperm, or perhaps anybody else's, may exacerbate competitive feelings and cause friction. This could be especially difficult in some families. Again, however, there has been no research on this aspect of donation and fertility problems.

Jealousy and envy

The use of either anonymous or known donor material may give rise to uncomfortable feelings of jealousy or envy. This may be directed at other fertile men or women in general, or specifically towards the known donor, or, in the case of semen donation, towards the partner who will be receiving, possibly for the first time, fertile sperm. The generalised feelings of resentment and jealousy towards others who are fertile may be reawakened or raised for the first time when confronted with the reality of using donor material. It is important for the counsellor to take the time to explore with the individual or couple what ambivalence they may have about the use of others' genetic material. In the case of known donation, while, as discussed earlier, the individual or couple may express a sense of relief and control about knowing the origin of the genetic material, there may also be an underlying discomfort, which is evidenced in such statements as, '*she* gets pregnant as easily as falling off a log', or 'he had no trouble getting *his* partner pregnant'. Such statements must be noticed and raised to overt discussion with the couple, since they may be assertions of angry or jealous feelings that may be masked behind the desire to convince the counsellor that these people's genetic material is really good and worth using.

Donation followed by no conception, or resulting in abnormal foetus or disabled child

Sometimes it is difficult for couples to envisage the possibility that there will be no conception. If the problem has been identified as the absence of sperm or ova, then it seems that the use of donated gametes will overcome this. In the case of donated semen, because the process of insemination is relatively simple, the notion that it may not 'work' immediately is hard to contemplate and difficult to understand. There are often high levels of expectation at the first insemination as the couple are convinced that it must result in conception. When it does not, the disappointment may be intense, and the couple confused and despairing. The dreadful possibility that there may be something 'wrong' with the woman may be raised. The disappointment when ovum donation 'fails' is as strong, but because there is obviously so much that can go wrong in the process, it may be true to say that couples who are having this form of treatment have a more realistic notion of the chances of conception. It may help them to manage their feelings if they know that the reality of donation means that conception is not guaranteed, that the processes involved in the use of donated gametes, that is, the freezing of semen, the timing of ovulation, the process of IVF, all mean that the pregnancy rates are low.

A difficult and painful area to explore is the possibility that the use of donated material may result, happily, in a pregnancy, but then that there is something wrong with the foetus, which may indicate a termination of that pregnancy, or that the baby is born with a disability of some kind.

For some, who have thought long and hard about whether they are able to accept a donor, this can confirm their worst fears about its use. They may feel that they have been 'justly punished' for not having accepted the situation as it was. When asked about the possibility of this occurring most couples will indicate that they are aware of the risks, which are generally the same as in the usual population (although there is a higher miscarriage rate with some of the techniques used), and are willing to go ahead. The special issues that arise, because they are using donated genetic material, need to be explored, if only briefly, so that they have the opportunity to discuss their awareness of their ambivalence in a safe environment. This will, it is hoped, mean that they will be more prepared and able to deal with the pain of such an outcome, should it occur.

The effect on the family relationships should the use of sibling-to-sibling donation result in no pregnancy, or in a baby who has special needs of some kind, is very hard to explore prior to the event. However, I believe that it is essential to do so, and in so doing the couples often begin to feel that they are really taking on what it means to enter this particular relationship, both with the potential child, and with the donor.

Case example

Pat and Paula were considering the use of Paula's sister's ova. Paula had always known and accepted that she was infertile. However, when the techniques that allow the use of donor ova became available, she realised that it might be possible to carry and give birth to a child after all. She and her partner had been very excited about this, but had two main concerns. First, they had understood from the clinic that if they found their own donor they would be able to move more quickly on to having the ovum donation done. They had understood this as meaning that they must use the donor that they found. After some discussion they realised that recruiting a donor on to the list, whether or not they used that donor's ova, meant movement up the waiting list anyway (as is the policy at many clinics). Secondly, Paula's sister Georgia had offered her eggs, and this offer was apparently well supported by the family.

> *Counsellor*: So your family is happy about this, is that right?
> *Paula*: Yes. They usually are about anything Georgia decides to do. [*Laughter.*]

The counsellor notices Paula's rather nervous laughter, and the statement clearly needs some further exploration, rather than taking it at face value.

> *Counsellor*: So Georgia often does what she wants to do?
> *Paula*: Oh yes. I mean, she's very nice and I am really grateful to her for offering. Once she decides to do something it is hard to stop her.

Counsellor: Now that you know that if Georgia is willing to donate her eggs to the list, if you like, and that you will move up the waiting list, does that make any difference to you?

Pat: Well, it does to me. I was willing to use Georgia's eggs if this was going to get things moving more quickly, but to be honest I was unhappy about it in some ways. She's quite a domineering sort of person, and people don't usually say no to her. I was worried that if this whole thing worked, we would be able to make it clear that the baby would be ours, and not hers.

Counsellor: This is important isn't it? You want to be able to feel that any baby was yours, and not that somehow it belonged elsewhere in the family.

Paula: Well, I think it would be ours, because I'd carry and give birth to it. But Pat is right. Georgia does interfere, and likes to be the centre of attention. I think it could be hard to keep her from interfering in our lives if she thought that somehow the baby was hers, or that we should be eternally grateful to her, meaning she could come round all the time or tell us what to do with the baby.

Counsellor: So where does this leave you now?

Pat: Well, I'd feel happier now that we've talked about it, to have an anonymous donor. It would seem more as though *we*, Paula and I, were doing this and not Georgia and the rest of the family too. If Georgia would be willing to give her eggs anyway, for the list, that'd be fine. If not, I'd be willing to recruit some donors from our area, and move up the list that way.

Counsellor: What about you Paula, how do you feel now?

Paula: I agree. This feels much better. I *was* worried about how it would work out. I like feeling that this is something that is personal for me and Pat, and not a family business somehow.

The counsellor here helps the couple to surface some of their concerns about the use of Georgia's ova, and what it might mean for them in relation not only to the family as a whole, but also to them as a new family. There is clearly some resentment about Georgia, and the session could move on to helping Paula and Pat to practise telling Georgia that they would not want to use her eggs themselves but would be happy for her to help them by donating to the general 'pool'. Some of the counsellor's work in this situation might be to help this couple to assert their 'couple-ness', in the face of strong family dynamics.

Case example

The following example shows in a more in-depth way the process of counselling a couple where the woman's sister will be donating the ova. To tell or not to tell the child is specifically focused on in this session.

Flora and Tom had heard four months previously that Flora's symptoms had been confirmed as premature menopause. Flora was now on hormone replacement therapy, but could not now have any hope of a genetic child of her own. Her sister, Maureen, who had three children, had offered her eggs to them.

Counsellor: I understand that you will be using your sister's eggs, is that right?

Tom: Yes. That's right.

Counsellor: What has been your thinking about whether to tell the child?

Flora: Yes. We wouldn't really have to worry about thinking about that aspect until the child is at least old enough to take it in, but it is still going to be a few years.

Tom: Our doctor said that we do not have to worry for about three years until the child sort of understands and then you, you obviously then, I suppose . . .

Here, Tom is unable to complete his sentence and stops, apparently in confusion.

Counsellor: I guess it is difficult to think so far ahead.

Tom: Yes, being a parent you feel differently to what you do now, you must think differently. So obviously when you're a parent you're going to have to tackle things better, so this isn't really a problem to think about in the short term but obviously long term you've definitely got to think about it.

Flora: I think I probably would tell the child. It depends on how everyone else is around us, if they've forgotten the whole thing. I've had the baby, I've given birth to it, I've breastfed it, they'll probably forget all about that it was even an egg donor. I think time will tell. I think we will tread that path nearer the time.

Although both Flora and Tom are addressing their remarks to the counsellor it is as though they are having this conversation together.

Tom: Both our parents have said that really there is no need to tell the child.

Flora: So we are just going to keep it to ourselves and that's it.

Counsellor: What I am hearing is that you are open to how you feel at the time. I wonder if it would be helpful to discuss this a little more? Perhaps to examine what others' experiences have been, to help you to clarify what you may want to do in the future?

Flora: Yes, I think so, as we haven't been there yet, it might help.

Counsellor: What you are dealing with here is that for the first time, over the last eight or nine years, it has been possible to separate the birth mother from the genetic mother and that's a very difficult idea for a lot of people. We don't really know what the effect of it is psychologically, either on the child, parents or the families. In terms of anonymity, telling or not telling the child, the general move seems to be towards openness and telling the child. This comes out of the adoption experience and the semen donation experience. Where children have been bought up knowing – never knowing a time then they were not aware of their special conception – it seems they tend to make a good adjustment. There is a lot yet that we don't know, and there must be many children out in the world who have never known about the circumstances of their conception, who are presumably also happy and well adjusted.

The counsellor is giving quite a lot of information here, and this is quite deliberate. She is wanting to offer the couple options to have in their minds, to help them choose as consciously as they can which course of action they will take. This is also an opportunity for each of them to voice any thoughts they have about this.

Tom: I think that to be told later on in life could be a bit of a shock. Our doctor actually said she advised us to tell the child, although she said there is no hurry. She said it is best to tell them and she said from about the age of 3.

Counsellor: Children will start asking all those awkward questions, about where they come from, and how did they get here, won't they? Have you thought about how you might respond to that?

Flora: I think I want to be as honest as possible, what about you Tom?

Tom: I think that I would rather tell the truth, in a way that a child would understand. That sort of thing is difficult for all parents, but keeping a secret about it would be difficult. I'm not very good at lying.

Flora: I think we definitely will say.

Tom: We come from quite an open family.

Counsellor: It sounds as though you have told your families about all that has happened, is that right?

Flora: Tom is probably not as close to his mum and dad as I am to my mum and dad. I've started to approach Tom's mum and dad in the same way as I approach my parents and they've been fine. Tom's been perhaps a bit shy himself and not been able to talk to them about the infertility problem. I think that they are very understanding though. I think that eventually, because everyone knows anyway, we will probably say something to the child.

Here the counsellor has given Flora and Tom room to verbalise their thoughts about whether to tell the child of its genetic origins. With very little active help the couple work through the situation that they are in and realise that because so many family members already know about their infertility and that they wish to use Flora's sister's ova, then it is probably unrealistic not to tell the child. They both also come to the realisation that they don't want to lie (as they see it) to the child. There is a noticeable shift from Flora's earlier statement, 'We'll just keep it to ourselves.'

The next part of the session deals with the feelings that Flora and Tom have about using Flora's sister's ova. Flora presented at the start of the session in a determinedly cheerful way. During the session, however, she begins every now and then to weep for a short time. As the counsellor gently begins to ask about their feelings on discovering that Flora had gone through a very early menopause at the age of 28, Flora looks very sad and begins to cry.

Flora: I couldn't believe it. I thought that I had lots of time to have a baby of my own.

Counsellor: How have you grieved about the fact that you are not going to have your own genetic child, however close your sister is to you? This is not going to be your genetic child.

Tom: I don't know, really. It was such a shock. Then Maureen said that she would donate to us, so I'm not sure we have really stopped since then to really feel what has happened. Flora cries a lot, so maybe it's me that hasn't felt it properly yet.

Counsellor: What difference does it make for you, Tom, that you will not be having a child that is genetically the result of both you and Flora?

Tom: Well, I am sad about it. I think that it is more important that we have a baby, though, and that the fact that Flora will carry the child and give birth to it is much more important than the genetic thing.

Flora: I feel involved in this which is a good thing. I am going to be able to carry the baby, hopefully, which is what I want.

Tom: That is what is really important I think. It has been a big strain, though, wondering if it is going to be possible at all, whether we will ever have children.

Counsellor: Let's look for a moment at the idea of not having children at all and what you might do about that. You've talked about adoption, or perhaps at some point, that you might be involved in raising children and how that may feel.

Tom: We want to be involved in bringing up children in some way or another and we wouldn't give up if this doesn't happen. It would take a bit of getting used to and I'd be sad that we hadn't had the experience of pregnancy and childbirth, but we'll deal with that if it happens.

Counsellor: I am hearing from you that although it is quite soon after you found out there was this major difficulty, you have done a lot of talking together. That is usually important and it seems you get a lot of help and comfort from each other. One of my roles is to ensure that you leave communication lines open to the people who are going to be able to support you, and you seem to be doing that. You have thought through some of the implications, you know what you are feeling at the moment and it sounds like it's a mixture of excitement, hope, sadness, grief and anger all mixed in together.

For this couple, the genetic link is not as important as being involved in the process of raising children, although there is, for them, some comfort in the knowledge that they know the origin of the genetic material that will be used. It is noticeable that the counsellor does not pursue the grief that has been touched upon here. She has allowed Flora and Tom to touch this and withdraw. Clearly they need to feel hope and to have a sense of direction. The counsellor moves on to discuss other options should the donation not result in a pregnancy. This helps to focus the couple in the reality that donation is not always successful, while at the same time recognising that they have other options in the future. The counsellor then chooses to summarise what has happened and to endorse positively how Flora and Tom are communicating together, how they support and care for each other. This positive endorsement is very helpful for many couples who compare themselves to others, and wonder if they are 'as good as' everyone else. The counsellor may be sensing here that this endorsement is needed, since Tom in particular seems to have suddenly gone into 'control' mode. The counsellor may defuse this, and thus allow room for some of the more confused and distressing feelings to have expression.

10

Counselling for Donors

The notion that counselling might be needed for donors had not been seriously considered until fairly recently, with the advent of oocyte donation. It may be that since semen donors, in Britain and elsewhere have traditionally been recruited from the medical student population, the need for counselling was not considered seriously. Some professionals, however, have always felt that donors should have the opportunity to speak with someone, apart from those concerned with the screening process that donors are required to undergo. The main emphasis has hitherto been on delivering a high quality 'product' to the consumer, that is the recipient person or couple, and thus much work has been done on the process of screening donors to exclude genetic disease and to assess fertility. However, with greater emphasis now being directed towards the welfare of the child generally, which in Britain is now enshrined in law with the Human Fertilisation and Embryology Act 1990 (see Appendix 1), there has come an increasing concern with the counselling needs of the donors, and with the assessment of *psychological* risk for both donors and any offspring.

This chapter will be concerned with the recruitment and screening of both semen and oocyte donors, and will explore and examine the counselling process involved.

Recruitment

Semen donors
In the early years of semen donation, pragmatism dictated that donors needed to be an easily available group, on site, and willing. Medical students fulfilled these criteria admirably, and although there has been discussion in some feminist literature about medical arrogance (surrounding the belief that women who receive this semen are getting a good deal *because* the donors were medical students), and while this may be true in some instances, it is probable that the reasons were very much more mundane than that.

The use of medical students has been common in Britain, while 'in Canada, 80 per cent of donors are students and this is usually the case in Spain. In the USA most doctors (62 per cent) use medical students or hospital residents' (Cusine, 1988/1990: 92). However, in France only married men 'under fifty with one or more normal children' (Cusine, 1988/1990: 92) are used as semen donors, and it appears that in those countries where the practice is to recruit from a wider population it has generally been successful in that the numbers of donors have not fallen significantly. The debate about whether semen donors *should* be recruited primarily from medical schools and universities, or whether they should come from a wider group with criteria based on marital status and proven fertility is not one that I wish to enter at length here. However, there would be clear differences in the context in which a young, single, undergraduate would donate as opposed to that in which a married man with two children would consider donation. The issue of his wife's consent to the donation would need to be considered, for example. Those in long-term partnerships where there may or may not be children would clearly need to be considered in a different way also. This then would influence the environment in which counselling would take place, and who may be involved. Is it just the single medical student, or is it the man and his wife or partner? Issues of anonymity are also thereby altered. This aspect will be discussed further later in this chapter.

Oocyte donors

These donors are often recruited through gynaecological units, and are sometimes women who are undergoing sterilisation or hysterectomy. Recruitment here is delicate since it is clearly essential that the women are not placed under any pressure to donate their eggs. The King's Fund Report on *Counselling for Regulated Fertility Treatments* states:

> It is important that persons approached to donate gametes or embryos are not in a situation where they may feel themselves to be under an obligation to comply with the wishes of the person making the approach. This could be the case where potential donors are also patients receiving treatment under the care of the person making the approach. (King's Fund, 1991: 15:4.3)

The report goes on to make the following recommendation: 'Care should be taken to ensure that potential donors do not feel themselves to be under an obligation to comply with the request to donate their gametes' (1991: 15).

This care is essential both for semen and oocyte donation when considering the use of donated gametes from a friend or relative, as well as in the case of women who are asked to donate when they are in the position of needing to have care or surgery from the person, department or clinic requesting this of them. The HFEA Code of Practice states clearly, 'The possibility of donating gametes or embryos should not be raised during a potential donor's treatment cycle. The possibility should be raised by someone other than the staff involved in the treatment' (1990: 3.ix).

One British study describes getting donors from various sources, including 'women undergoing sterilisation procedures, friends or relatives of recipients prepared to make known donations and fertile volunteers prepared to undergo ovarian stimulation and oocyte collection to provide eggs to anonymous recipients . . . Media coverage of ovum donation has resulted in 30 fertile women volunteering to donate oocytes for the programme' (Power et al., 1990: 352).

Unlike semen donation, where donors are often single and do not usually have children of their own, clinics recruiting oocyte donors face a rather different situation. In one unit in England for example it is usual for any ovum donor to have had the family that she wants and not to consider donation until she has had her children. In the same study, conducted in 1990 and quoted above, 85 per cent of donors had had one or more children, with only 15% not having had any children (Power et al., 1990: 353). This undoubtedly reflects the fact that the procedures for donating eggs have greater risks attached to them than that for donating semen, and that if a woman is wanting to have children it is best not to put herself or her fertility at risk by donating eggs until she has done so.

Screening procedures

For both semen and ovum donors the medical screening covers family, genetic and medical history, and a variety of tests to ensure fertility. Potential donors must be made aware that the results of tests may be given to them and what this implies, for example in the case of HIV infection. Most legislation already covers the age at which donors are legally allowed to donate, and some countries have specific guidelines as to the age *after* which donation should not be considered. The HFEA Code of Practice states that 'Gametes should not be taken for the treatment of others from female donors over the age of 35, and from male donors over the age of 55, unless there are exceptional reasons for doing so' (HFEA, 1990: 3.vii). Clear information and an opportunity to ask questions about the tests are important. An example of a leaflet published by the HFEA in 1992 concentrating on the legal aspects is reproduced in the Appendices.

The counselling process
For the purposes of this book it is necessary to concentrate on the reasons for counselling donors, and how this counselling may be seen as part of the screening process.

For many counsellors the use of the word 'counselling' is inappropriate when considering its use in screening donors. This raises the question discussed more fully in Chapter 1 about the context of counselling. I think that it *is* appropriate to offer counselling to donors before they commit themselves to donating their genetic material as this gives them the chance to air concerns that they may have, and offers the counsellor the opportunity to ensure that the social and legal implications of donation have been fully explored. How that counselling is perceived by the potential donor is an issue which counsellors need to raise, and the limits of such counselling need also to be clearly defined.

Useful questions for the counsellor

- What concerns, if any, do you have about donating your sperm/eggs?
- What are the reasons that you are considering donating your sperm/eggs?
- Who else knows that you are considering donating your eggs/sperm?
- How do you feel about not knowing the outcome of your donation?

The first question, as to what concerns a donor might have about the process or implications of donating, allows donors to explore their anxieties. This question may bring to light, for example, a semen donor's worries about his fertility or a concern that if he is tested for HIV infection this may have implications for future insurance, or medical care.

For an oocyte donor, this question may show a worry over future fertility. Even if she currently is sure that she has enough children, there may be anxieties about having options open later for further children. Some are anxious that their eggs or sperm only go to particular *kinds* of recipients. This decision will usually be the province of the clinic, although some units may allow a certain level of control, even over 'altruistic' donation to the gamete 'pool'.

Case example

Bill, a 22-year-old postgraduate business school student attended the DI clinic for donor screening. When asked what had brought him to consider sperm donation he said that some of his friends had done it, and that it seemed like an easy thing to do to help people. He also admitted that he was curious to see if he was fertile.

Counsellor: Is there any reason to suppose that you might not be?
Bill: Not really. I think it would be interesting to know, that's all.
Counsellor: Are there any particular concerns that you have about donating your sperm?
Bill: No. Obviously I wouldn't want a child turning up on my doorstep in sixteen or eighteen years time, but I see that you keep this confidential.
Counsellor: Yes. There are only rare cases where that confidentiality may be broken as you have seen in the information that you have had. So long as you are as open with us about your medical and family history as possible, there should be no problems of that nature in the future. Is there any one else who knows that you are considering being a sperm donor?
Bill: Yes, some of my friends do. They already do it, some here and some at another centre. It seems to be easy enough and it's just like giving blood really. I am a blood donor, and I don't really see a difference. Obviously it *is* a bit different, but it's not a difficult or painful thing to do, and it is a shame if people can't have children I think. I want them later and it would be hard if I couldn't.
Counsellor: Is that one of the reasons also that you want to do this, to check your own fertility out, so that you don't have to worry about that in the future?
Bill: I guess so, but as well as that I think it is a good idea to do it.
Counsellor: All right, there may be some further questions that you have after you have seen the doctor, so we'll meet again then just to be sure that you are quite comfortable about this.

The counsellor's task here is gently to question Bill to ensure that he is aware of *his* motivation to donate, and to raise to conscious awareness issues that are of concern, in this case Bill's concern about his own fertility. Should the medical screening raise any further issues, perhaps about HIV or other infection risks, previous surgery or injury or doubts about family medical history, then there is the opportunity for Bill to see the counsellor again. The availability of the counsellor is also important if it is found that Bill has any fertility problem that shows in his semen analysis.

Returning to the list of questions above, the next concerns motivation for donating. This question is probably of more concern to outside observers than to those who are involved in this process. It seems that people who wish to donate *generally* wish to do so from a sense of helping others to have a family. In the case of egg donors there is often a real desire to enable another woman to have a child, and experience that which has been so important for the donor, that is, parenthood. In a British study looking at attitudes of donors to their donation, in answer to the question 'Why did you donate eggs?' 95 per cent of volunteers and 93 per cent of infertile donors (that is, those who were undergoing treatment on the assisted conception programme and whose treatment resulted in 'spare' oocytes) replied that they did so 'to help another'. Of the infertile donors, 7 per cent made the donation to check their fertility, and 5 per cent did so at the time that they were sterilised (Power et al., 1990: 353). Although the numbers in this study are small (total 35), the responses are interesting and fit with anecdotal evidence and experience.

For semen donors this is also often the motivation. They may have a friend who has had problems conceiving, or fathering a child, and see semen donation as certainly no more difficult (and more pleasant) than giving blood. These semen donors generally do understand that the implications of donating genetic material are rather more long lasting, usually, than giving blood. However, it is also true to say that semen donors, usually coming from an impecunious student life, are often partially motivated at least by the expenses fees paid to them for their donations.

The counsellor's role here is, in effect, to assess the way in which the potential donor views the act of donating their genetic material, in an effort to prevent those people from donating for whom the psychological sequelae may be damaging.

Case example

Emily, a woman of 34, attended the clinic, after there had been a series of articles and programmes in the media about the new technologies and the possibility of having children through ovum donation. In these articles etc. notice had been drawn to the need for ovum donors. Emily had travelled a long distance and had attended alone. The counsellor saw her after she had had an interview with the doctor who had raised some concerns and had wanted to ensure that Emily did, in fact, see a counsellor. In the history that the doctor had taken, two facts were seen by the counsellor to be important and worth further exploration. First, that Emily had had two abortions within the past three years, apparently by choice under the legislation, that is they were not spontaneous abortions. Secondly, that Emily was currently in a relationship, that had begun and lasted over that period of three years. She was not married, and had no children. The counsellor's concerns were focused on the awareness that most egg donors have had children, or at least made a clear decision not to have any children, and that two terminations of pregnancy within the past three years *might* indicate some ambivalence about fertility or motherhood. The counsellor was also concerned to ascertain the role of Emily's relationship with her partner as Emily saw it (the partner not having attended the appointment), both in the abortions and in this wish to be a donor. The relationship may or may not have been a factor in this desire to donate.

The counsellor gently asked Emily about these abortions and Emily replied that she had had them because the relationship was not a good one in which to bring up children. She said that she had no regrets about them and merely wished to not waste her eggs any further and allow someone else to have them, who could give them a good home.

> *Counsellor*:   So it is important to you that whoever gets your eggs is capable of looking after any children that might result. Is that right?
> *Emily*:   Yes, I wouldn't want anyone to mistreat them at all.
> *Counsellor*:   [*taking a risk by interpreting what Emily has said*] I wonder, Emily, if donating your eggs is a way for you to feel that you have children somewhere, who are looked after in the way that you were not able to look after the two pregnancies that you have had?
> *Emily*:   [*suddenly crying*] It seems so wrong, what I did, I can make it up this way.

The counsellor then went on working for a short while with Emily, to help her to accept a referral for post-abortion counselling, and to delay donating her eggs until she had resolved the issues that she had from these abortions and within her relationship. It seemed likely that Emily's desire to be a donor could be a statement of independence from the relationship. 'You can't stop me from having children in some way or another.' These very painful issues needed to be worked with before any further decision could be made about egg donation.

Here the counsellor is making an assessment, not as to the *suitability* of Emily as an egg donor, but as to the *appropriateness* of this as a way of resolving her guilt and grief, and frustrated desire for a child of her own. Emily's well-being and issues raised are the counsellor's concern. The counsellor's approach to Emily is as someone who is thinking about Emily's pain and anxieties, not whether she is suitable to donate from the recipient's viewpoint. This distinction is an important one and one that the counsellor is uniquely placed to manage.

The third question, 'Who else knows that you are considering donating your eggs/sperm?', helps the counsellor to ensure that any donor has the support he or she needs in order to do this. In the case of egg donors, the woman is usually married with children, and her husband needs to give his consent. Married sperm donors' wives also need formally to consent. For egg donors the procedures necessary for the donation are equivalent to IVF, and thus require some support at home from the family or partner. Thus most egg donors will have told someone else about the desire or intention to donate.

In the same study discussed above (Power et al., 1990), 95 per cent of volunteer donors and 73 per cent of infertile donors had told someone else about the donation. The volunteer donors had told a friend (75 per cent), GP (65 per cent) and/or parent (50 per cent). The infertile donors had told a friend and/or relative (46 per cent each), and significantly fewer had told a parent or GP (1990: 353). This probably reflects their infertile status and their desire to keep this hidden from parents, at least for the moment.

The counsellor's role here is to work with donors to help them to have the support they need, to give information about the social and legal aspects of the donation process, and to help them to be as certain as they can that they are comfortable with what they are planning.

The fourth question, 'How do you feel about not knowing the outcome of your donation' is a useful one that helps the donor to clarify his or her motivation to donate. Are they wishing to check out their fertility? Are they wanting to enact a fantasy of 'super-stud' or 'fertility goddess' (both of these rare in my experience)? More importantly, are they likely to suffer from such uncomfortable curiosity about their possible genetic offspring that they might become driven to find out more information about them? If this is the case, what is the significance of donating their genetic material, and can this significant need be met, or managed, more appropriately?

In the case of Emily, the counsellor did not need to ask this question, as Emily volunteered this information in her statement about wanting to give her eggs a 'good home', and not wanting them to be 'mistreated at all'. This was a clear indication to the counsellor that Emily may have been over-invested in the fate of her eggs.

Anonymity

The importance of this for both donors and recipients is an interesting area of study. Both egg and sperm donors, in Britain, are required to give some identifying information to the licensed clinic, so that this information can be passed on to the HFEA. This is so that the Authority can hold a register of donors for children who know, or suspect that they are, the result of gamete donation to be able to check that they are not hoping to have a child with someone who is their genetic half-sibling. The idea of accidental 'incest' produces anxiety, and this process is designed to relieve those fears as well as to help future children. The only way in which a child might learn the name of the person who donated their genetic material is if there was a case to answer in relation to the donor withholding information about an inherited disease, and the child was wishing to sue for damages (see Appendix 4: *Sperm and Egg Donors and the Law*).

Attitudes to anonymity held by donors and by recipients have not been studied extensively. However, there appear to be a number of interesting differences that have been pointed to and which warrant brief discussion here.

It seems that recipients are less open to the idea of contact between the donor and any child when the child has grown up than are donors. In the little published research available, it seems that when asked, 'Would you object if the child/donor made contact when an adult?', 46 per cent of donors and 88 per cent of recipients said yes. Of further interest is that when asked, 'If you were born of a donated egg, would you want to know the donor?', 56 per cent of donors said no, but 86 per cent of recipients said no (Kirkland et al., 1992: 356).

It would appear from this that recipients of donated gametes frame their answers from a viewpoint that protects themselves from overt acknowledgement of their infertility. This is not the same as saying that recipients are unwilling to tell the child that they are the result of gamete donation, only that they seem, in advance of the real situation, to be reluctant to have a potential 'parent' threaten their own, hard-fought, role as parents.

Most semen donors donate anonymously and seem to want it to be this way. If known donation is needed for any reason, this can be, and often is, done outside the clinic setting. Thus attitudes to known donation amongst these donors are less well researched. However, the responses of recipients to semen donation seem to be much the same as those who are recipients of egg donation, that is, they are not comfortable, in general, with the idea that the donor and the child may have contact in the future. This whole area needs considerable research before we are able to understand more fully what the issues are, and thus perhaps to modify not only legislation if necessary, but also counselling approaches, to take further account of donors' needs and motivations.

Case example

The following is an in-depth case example of working with an egg donor who is considering donating to her sister.

> *Counsellor*: I understand that you want to donate to your sister. Tell me a little bit about how all that came about.

The counsellor begins with an open-ended question to help Ann to tell the story in her own way.

> *Ann*: Well, my sister's been married nearly three years. She has been trying for a baby for two years. She kept getting pregnancy tests which were negative. Then she thought perhaps there was a problem, and had consultations with different people. Just before Christmas last year she was told that she was going through her menopause, and she was just devastated. She's only 26 years old. I've recently had a baby in November, and so I felt terrible too.

The counsellor does not yet pick this statement up, but notes it since this may be relevant in the motivation that Ann has to help her sister.

> *Counsellor*: Oh, so you've just had a baby?
> *Ann*: Yes, I've got a baby. Anyway, she went further and she was told about egg donation. We discussed it and I thought that that's the best I can do for her. She really wants a baby and I've had one. Obviously, I want more children but having that baby, knowing how wonderful he is, I thought I've got to do it.
> *Counsellor*: You want to be able to give her the chance, is that right?
> *Ann*: Yes. I do.
> *Counsellor*: Have you talked this over with anyone apart from your sister?

The counsellor is checking what support Ann has available as well as the attitudes of those around her.

> *Ann*: Yes, I have. My husband has been great about it.
> *Counsellor*: Can you say how he feels about this?

> *Ann*: He says that as long as there are no risks and that I will feel
> OK afterwards, then to do it. He's happy about it. All of us,
> everyone, the whole family, parents as well have discussed it.
>
> *Counsellor*: So the whole family is aware of what's happening?
>
> *Ann*: Yes, my dad's fine about it, but he said no one else needs to
> know about this. He said not to tell everyone, that this is between us.
>
> *Counsellor*: What do you think about that?
>
> *Ann*: Well, I think he's right really. It really only concerns us.

It is becoming clearer that although the family of the two sisters are
supportive, there is a desire that this whole process is kept private.
How this will affect the child, the donor and her husband and child
and other relatives later is important and needs to be raised.

> *Counsellor*: How have you and Lisa decided that you might explain
> this to any child that may be born?
>
> *Ann*: Well we weren't going to. We think it would be best once I've
> given her the egg, then just carry on as usual. I don't think that she
> will tell the child.
>
> *Counsellor*: Do you anticipate that as being easy to do or is that
> going to be quite difficult?
>
> *Ann*: I don't think it's going to be easy but we are very close and I
> think that what's made me want to do this. We have talked about it
> a lot and, it's hard to explain, I'd feel happy to do it for her, but it
> will be difficult I know.
>
> *Counsellor*: Can you tell me what you think will be difficult about it
> for you?

The counsellor brings the discussion to what this means for Ann
the donor, rather than Ann, the sister who wants to help.

> *Ann*: I know it's complicated, and it's weird and difficult. I think once
> those eggs are taken out, then it's up to her. I know I've just got to
> do it for her. I think it is entirely up to Lisa whatever she wants. As
> far as I am concerned she is going to be the mother so it's entirely
> up to her.

The counsellor is aware here that Ann has not directly answered the
question about what would be difficult for her. Ann seems to be
getting more determined to help her sister, and in the counselling
session is perhaps becoming a little anxious that she may not be
able to. The counsellor frames the next statement in terms of
possible effects on Ann and her immediate family, as a way of
enabling Ann to focus on herself a little more.

> *Counsellor*: That's right. Yet this may have an effect on you and your
> children. In a way you will be your sister's child's aunt as well as its
> genetic mother. Your children will be its cousins as well as its genetic
> half-siblings. What do you feel about that?
>
> *Ann*: Well, it's a bit strange put like that, but I think that if I had any
> worries in my mind then I wouldn't be here. You know, she's only

young and I just feel that to do this for her would be great. I think it would be different if I didn't have a child but having him just makes me realise how nice it is and how difficult it probably is for her to see me with him.

Counsellor: You are wanting to do this for her and I understand that. It feels like a very sisterly and loving thing to do. I guess it's important not to feel too badly if it doesn't work and also not to feel badly because you have a child and she doesn't. Does that make sense to you?

Ann: Yes, it does. I think if it doesn't work I may always feel a bit guilty that it didn't, although I will have done what I could, and certainly sad that she hadn't got children.

Counsellor: So if it works or doesn't work, in a sense that's for her to deal with. You'll feel sad because she's your sister and she's not getting pregnant?

Ann: That's right, I would, I would feel for her. But I wouldn't think, it's my fault or anything like that. Although it's hard to believe that it might not work. We are all so excited about it.

Counsellor: Do you think your family is counting on this working?

Ann: Yes, they're really excited. They really want this to happen. They know it's not a certainty though. We've all talked about this on many occasions but they are really happy about it. They say that's the best gift I could give her.

Counsellor: Is that how it feels, that it is a gift?

Ann: Yes, that is exactly how it feels.

The counsellor has explored with Ann her feelings about donating to her sister and the impact this may have on her, her family and the family of origin. There seems to be a strong desire to do what she can to help her sister, which is quite powerful and overrides concerns that she has about the procedures. The counsellor accepts that this is syntonic within the family and does not press her any further. This would be going into deeper therapeutic waters which Ann has not agreed to enter. The counsellor's role is to ensure that Ann has sufficient information and free space within the session to feel that she has explored the issues that are important to her, to enable her to make a choice that rests comfortably with her. Further work within this session would be to ensure as far as possible that Ann has considered other areas of concern, such as her own future fertility should she want to have more children herself, and the risks involved in the egg donation procedures. These risks are usually discussed with the medical team, but there may need to be room to air any feelings about them.

Counselling donors involves the same skills discussed in Chapter 2 in the consideration of Egan's helping model. The stages of

Exploration and New Understanding are the most relevant ones, using the skills of giving attention, listening and helping the client be specific, as well as giving information and recognising themes and inconsistencies. It is unlikely to be relevant within the clinic setting that sperm or egg donors will need further work that would fall within Egan's stage 3 of Action. The task of the counsellor is to act as a filter through which the concerns and anxieties of donors may be heard and appropriately managed. Should there be difficulties and pain that donors bring with them and which are being channelled into the act of donation, as in the case example of Emily given earlier in this chapter, then it is the counsellor's role to help the donor to make that process overt and to refer appropriately to on-going counselling or psychotherapy, as and if necessary.

Appendix 1

Human Fertilisation and Embryology Act 1990: Chapter 37

1a   Arrangement of Sections

Principal terms used

47. Index.
48. Northern Ireland.
49. Short title, commencement, etc.

Schedules:
Schedule 1—The Authority: supplementary provisions.
Schedule 2—Activities for which licences may be granted.
Schedule 3—Consents to use of gametes or embryos.
Schedule 4—Status: amendments of enactments.

A copy of the Act and the relevant schedules is available through Her Majesty's Stationery Office. Extracts from the Act are given in Appendix 1b and Schedule 3 is reproduced in Appendix 1c.

1b   Excerpts from Chapter 37

An Act to make provision in connection with human embryos and any subsequent development of such embryos; to prohibit certain practices in connection with embryos and gametes; to establish a Human Fertilisation and Embryology Authority; to make provision about the persons who in certain circumstances are to be treated in law as the parents of a child; and to amend the Surrogacy Arrangements Act 1985. [1st November 1990]

. . .

Principal terms used

1.—(1) In this Act, except where otherwise stated—

    (a) embryo means a live human embryo where fertilisation is complete, and

    (b) references to an embryo include an egg in the process of fertilisation,

and, for this purpose, fertilisation is not complete until the appearance of a two cell zygote.

Meaning of 'embryo', 'gamete' and associated expressions.

(2) This Act, so far as it governs bringing about the creation of an embryo, applies only to bringing about the creation of an embryo outside the human body; and in this Act—

    (a) references to embryos the creation of which was brought about *in vitro* (in their application to those where fertilisation is complete) are to those where fertilisation began outside the human body whether or not it was completed there, and

    (b) references to embryos taken from a woman do not include embryos whose creation was brought about *in vitro*.

(3) This Act, so far as it governs the keeping or use of an embryo, applies only to keeping or using an embryo outside the human body.

(4) References in this Act to gametes, eggs or sperm, except where otherwise stated, are to live human gametes, eggs or sperm but references below in this Act to gametes or eggs do not include eggs in the process of fertilisation.

. . .

Activities governed by the Act

Prohibitions in connection with embryos.

3.—(1) No person shall—

(a) bring about the creation of an embryo, or

(b) keep or use an embryo,

except in pursuance of a licence.

(2) No person shall place in a woman—

(a) a live embryo other than a human embryo, or

(b) any live gametes other than human gametes.

(3) A licence cannot authorise—

(a) keeping or using an embryo after the appearance of the primitive streak,

(b) placing an embryo in any animal,

(c) keeping or using an embryo in any circumstances in which regulations prohibit its keeping or use, or

(d) replacing a nucleus of a cell of an embryo with a nucleus taken from a cell of any person, embryo or subsequent development of an embryo.

(4) For the purposes of subsection (3)(a) above, the primitive streak is to be taken to have appeared in an embryo not later than the end of the period of 14 days beginning with the day when the gametes are mixed, not counting any time during which the embryo is stored.

Prohibitions in connection with gametes.

4.—(1) No person shall—

(a) store any gametes, or

(b) in the course of providing treatment services for any woman, use the sperm of any man unless the services are being provided for the woman and the man together or use the eggs of any other woman, or

(c) mix gametes with the live gametes of any animal,

except in pursuance of a licence.

(2) A licence cannot authorise storing or using gametes in any circumstances in which regulations prohibit their storage or use.

(3) No person shall place sperm and eggs in a woman in any circumstances specified in regulations except in pursuance of a licence.

(4) Regulations made by virtue of subsection (3) above may provide that, in relation to licences only to place sperm and eggs in a woman in such circumstances, sections 12 to 22 of this Act shall have effect with such modifications as may be specified in the regulations.

(5) Activities regulated by this section or section 3 of this Act are referred to in this Act as 'activities governed by this Act'.

. . .

14.—(1) The following shall be conditions of every licence authorising the storage of gametes or embryos—   Conditions of storage licences.

   (a) that gametes of a person or an embryo taken from a woman shall be placed in storage only if received from that person or woman or acquired from a person to whom a licence applies and that an embryo the creation of which has been brought about *in vitro* otherwise than in pursuance of that licence shall be placed in storage only if acquired from a person to whom a licence applies,

   (b) that gametes or embryos which are or have been stored shall not be supplied to a person otherwise than in the course of providing treatment services unless that person is a person to whom a licence applies,

   (c) that no gametes or embryos shall be kept in storage for longer than the statutory storage period and, if stored at the end of the period, shall be allowed to perish, and

   (d) that such information as the Authority may specify in directions as to the persons whose consent is required under Schedule 3 to this Act, the terms of their consent and the circumstances of the storage and as to such other matters as the Authority may specify in directions shall be included in the records maintained in pursuance of the licence.

(2) No information shall be removed from any records maintained in pursuance of such a licence before the expiry of such period as may be specified in directions for records of the class in question.

(3) The statutory storage period in respect of gametes is such period not exceeding ten years as the licence may specify.

(4) The statutory storage period in respect of embryos is such period not exceeding five years as the licence may specify.

(5) Regulations may provide that subsection (3) or (4) above shall have effect as if for ten years or, as the case may be, five years there were substituted—

(a) such shorter period, or

(b) in such circumstances as may be specified in the regulations, such longer period,

as may be specified in the regulations.

. . .

Code of practice.   **25.**—(1) The Authority shall maintain a code of practice giving guidance about the proper conduct of activities carried on in pursuance of a licence under this Act and the proper discharge of the functions of the person responsible and other persons to whom the licence applies.

(2) The guidance given by the code shall include guidance for those providing treatment services about the account to be taken of the welfare of children who may be born as a result of treatment services (including a child's need for a father), and of other children who may be affected by such births.

(3) The code may also give guidance about the use of any technique involving the placing of sperm and eggs in a woman.

(4) The Authority may from time to time revise the whole or any part of the code.

(5) The Authority shall publish the code as for the time being in force.

(6) A failure on the part of any person to observe any provision of the code shall not of itself render the person liable to any proceedings, but—

(a) a licence committee shall, in considering whether there has been any failure to comply with any conditions of a licence and, in particular, conditions requiring anything to be 'proper' or 'suitable', take account of any relevant provision of the code, and

(b) a licence committee may, in considering, where it has power to do so, whether or not to vary or revoke a licence, take into account any observance of or failure to observe the provisions of the code.

. . .

Status

Meaning of 'mother'.   **27.**—(1) The woman who is carrying or has carried a child as a result of the placing in her of an embryo or of sperm and eggs, and no other woman, is to be treated as the mother of the child.

(2) Subsection (1) above does not apply to any child to the extent that the child is treated by virtue of adoption as not being the child of any person other than the adopter or adopters.

(3) Subsection (1) above applies whether the woman was in the United Kingdom or elsewhere at the time of the placing in her of the embryo or the sperm and eggs.

28.—(1) This section applies in the case of a child who is being or has been carried by a woman as the result of the placing in her of an embryo or of sperm and eggs or her artificial insemination.

Meaning of 'father'.

(2) If—

(a) at the time of the placing in her of the embryo or the sperm and eggs or of her insemination, the woman was a party to a marriage, and

(b) the creation of the embryo carried by her was not brought about with the sperm of the other party to the marriage,

then, subject to subsection (5) below, the other party to the marriage shall be treated as the father of the child unless it is shown that he did not consent to the placing in her of the embryo or the sperm and eggs or to her insemination (as the case may be).

(3) If no man is treated, by virtue of subsection (2) above, as the father of the child but—

(a) the embryo or the sperm and eggs were placed in the woman, or she was artificially inseminated, in the course of treatment services provided for her and a man together by a person to whom a licence applies, and

(b) the creation of the embryo carried by her was not brought about with the sperm of that man,

then, subject to subsection (5) below, that man shall be treated as the father of the child.

(4) Where a person is treated as the father of the child by virtue of subsection (2) or (3) above, no other person is to be treated as the father of the child.

(5) Subsections (2) and (3) above do not apply—

(a) in relation to England and Wales and Northern Ireland, to any child who, by virtue of the rules of common law, is treated as the legitimate child of the parties to a marriage,

(b) in relation to Scotland, to any child who, by virtue of any enactment or other rule of law, is treated as the child of the parties to a marriage, or

(c) to any child to the extent that the child is treated by virtue of adoption as not being the child of any person other than the adopter or adopters.

(6) Where—

(a) the sperm of a man who had given such consent as is required by paragraph 5 of Schedule 3 to this Act was used for a purpose for which such consent was required, or

(b) the sperm of a man, or any embryo the creation of which was brought about with his sperm, was used after his death,

he is not to be treated as the father of the child.

(7) The references in subsection (2) above to the parties to a marriage at the time there referred to—

(a) are to the parties to a marriage subsisting at that time, unless a judicial separation was then in force, but

(b) include the parties to a void marriage if either or both of them reasonably believed at that time that the marriage was valid; and for the purposes of this subsection it shall be presumed, unless the contrary is shown, that one of them reasonably believed at that time that the marriage was valid.

(8) This section applies whether the woman was in the United Kingdom or elsewhere at the time of the placing in her of the embryo or the sperm and eggs or her artificial insemination.

(9) In subsection (7)(a) above, 'judicial separation' includes a legal separation obtained in a country outside the British Islands and recognised in the United Kingdom.

Effect of sections 27 and 28.

29.—(1) Where by virtue of section 27 or 28 of this Act a person is to be treated as the mother or father of a child, that person is to be treated in law as the mother or, as the case may be, father of the child for all purposes.

(2) Where by virtue of section 27 or 28 of this Act a person is not to be treated as the mother or father of a child, that person is to be treated in law as not being the mother or, as the case may be, father of the child for any purpose.

(3) Where subsection (1) or (2) above has effect, references to any relationship between two people in any enactment, deed or other instrument or document (whenever passed or made) are to be read accordingly.

(4) In relation to England and Wales and Northern Ireland, nothing in the provisions of section 27(1) or 28(2) to (4), read with this section, affects—

(a) the succession to any dignity or title of honour or renders any person capable of succeeding to or transmitting a right to succeed to any such dignity or title, or

(b) the devolution of any property limited (expressly or not) to devolve (as nearly as the law permits) along with any dignity or title of honour.

(5) In relation to Scotland—

(a) those provisions do not apply to any title, coat of arms, honour or dignity transmissible on the death of the holder thereof or affect the succession thereto or the devolution thereof, and

(b) where the terms of any deed provide that any property or interest in property shall devolve along with a title, coat of arms, honour or dignity, nothing in those provisions shall prevent that property or interest from so devolving.

30.—(1) The court may make an order providing for a child to be treated in law as the child of the parties to a marriage (referred to in this section as 'the husband' and 'the wife') if—

Parental orders in favour of gamete donors.

(a) the child has been carried by a woman other than the wife as the result of the placing in her of an embryo or sperm and eggs or her artificial insemination,

(b) the gametes of the husband or the wife, or both, were used to bring about the creation of the embryo, and

(c) the conditions in subsections (2) to (7) below are satisfied.

(2) The husband and the wife must apply for the order within six months of the birth of the child or, in the case of a child born before the coming into force of this Act, within six months of such coming into force.

(3) At the time of the application and of the making of the order—

(a) the child's home must be with the husband and the wife, and

(b) the husband or the wife, of both of them, must be domiciled in a part of the United Kingdom or in the Channel Islands or the Isle of Man.

(4) At the time of the making of the order both the husband and the wife must have attained the age of eighteen.

(5) The court must be satisfied that both the father of the child (including a person who is the father by virtue of section 28 of this Act), where he is not the husband, and the woman who carried the child have freely, and with full understanding of what is involved, agreed unconditionally to the making of the order.

(6) Subsection (5) above does not require the agreement of a person who cannot be found or is incapable of giving agreement and the agreement of the woman who carried the child is ineffective

for the purposes of that subsection if given by her less than six weeks after the child's birth.

(7) The court must be satisfied that no money or other benefit (other than for expenses reasonably incurred) has been given or received by the husband or the wife for or in consideration of—

    (a) the making of the order,

    (b) any agreement required by subsection (5) above,

    (c) the handing over of the child to the husband and the wife, or

    (d) the making of any arrangements with a view to the making of the order,

unless authorised by the court.

. . .

(9) Regulations may provide—

    (a) for any provision of the enactments about adoption to have effect, with such modifications (if any) as may be specified in the regulations, in relation to orders under this section, and applications for such orders, as it has effect in relation to adoption, and applications for adoption orders, and

    (b) for references in any enactment to adoption, an adopted child or an adoptive relationship to be read (respectively) as references to the effect of an order under this section, a child to whom such an order applies and a relationship arising by virtue of the enactments about adoption, as applied by the regulations, and for similar expressions in connection with adoption to be read accordingly,

and the regulations may include such incidental or supplemental provision as appears to the Secretary of State necessary or desirable in consequence of any provision made by virtue of paragraph (a) or (b) above.

1976 c. 36.
1978 c. 28.
S.I. 1987/2203
(N.I. 22).

(10) In this section 'the enactments about adoption' means the Adoption Act 1976, the Adoption (Scotland) Act 1978 and the Adoption (Northern Ireland) Order 1987.

(11) Subsection (1)(a) above applies whether the woman was in the United Kingdom or elsewhere at the time of the placing in her of the embryo or the sperm and eggs or her artificial insemination.

Information

The Authority's register of information.

31.—(1) The Authority shall keep a register which shall contain any information obtained by the Authority which falls within subsection (2) below.

(2) Information falls within this subsection if it relates to—

(a) the provision of treatment services for any identifiable individual, or

(b) the keeping or use of the gametes of any identifiable individual or of an embryo taken from any identifiable woman,

or if it shows that any identifiable individual was, or may have been, born in consequence of treatment services.

(3) A person who has attained the age of eighteen ('the applicant') may by notice to the Authority require the Authority to comply with a request under subsection (4) below, and the Authority shall do so if—

(a) the information contained in the register shows that the applicant was, or may have been, born in consequence of treatment services, and

(b) the applicant has been given a suitable opportunity to receive proper counselling about the implications of compliance with the request.

(4) The applicant may request the Authority to give the applicant notice stating whether or not the information contained in the register shows that a person other than a parent of the applicant would or might, but for sections 27 to 29 of this Act, be a parent of the applicant and, if it does show that—

(a) giving the applicant so much of that information as relates to the person concerned as the Authority is required by regulations to give (but no other information), or

(b) stating whether or not that information shows that, but for sections 27 to 29 of this Act, the applicant, and a person specified in the request as a person whom the applicant proposes to marry, would or might be related.

(5) Regulations cannot require the Authority to give any information as to the identity of a person whose gametes have been used or from whom an embryo has been taken if a person to whom a licence applied was provided with the information at a time when the Authority could not have been required to give information of the kind in question.

(6) A person who has not attained the age of eighteen ('the minor') may by notice to the Authority specifying another person ('the intended spouse') as a person whom the minor proposes to marry require the Authority to comply with a request under subsection (7) below, and the Authority shall do so if—

(a) the information contained in the register shows that the minor was, or may have been, born in consequence of treatment services, and

(b) the minor has been given a suitable opportunity to receive proper counselling about the implications of compliance with the request.

(7) The minor may request the Authority to give the minor notice stating whether or not the information contained in the register shows that, but for sections 27 to 29 of this Act, the minor and the intended spouse would or might be related.

Information to be provided to Registrar General.

32.—(1) This section applies where a claim is made before the Registrar General that a man is or is not the father of a child and it is necessary or desirable for the purpose of any function of the Registrar General to determine whether the claim is or may be well-founded.

(2) The Authority shall comply with any request made by the Registrar General by notice to the Authority to disclose whether any information on the register kept in pursuance of section 31 of this Act tends to show that the man may be the father of the child by virtue of section 28 of this Act and, if it does, disclose that information.

(3) In this section and section 33 of this Act, 'the Registrar General' means the Registrar General for England and Wales, the Registrar General of Births, Deaths and Marriages for Scotland or the Registrar General for Northern Ireland, as the case may be.

. . .

1984 c. 35.

(8) At the end of Part IV of the Data Protection Act 1984 (Exemptions) there is inserted—

'Information about human embryos, etc.

35A. Personal data consisting of information showing that an identifiable individual was, or may have been, born in consequence of treatment services (within the meaning of the Human Fertilisation and Embryology Act 1990) are exempt from the subject access provisions except so far as their disclosure under those provisions is made in accordance with section 31 of that Act (the Authority's register of information).'

Disclosure in interests of justice.

34.—(1) Where in any proceedings before a court the question whether a person is or is not the parent of a child by virtue of sections 27 to 29 of this Act falls to be determined, the court may on the application of any party to the proceedings make an order requiring the Authority—

(a) to disclose whether or not any information relevant to that question is contained in the register kept in pursuance of section 31 of this Act, and

(b) if it is, to disclose so much of it as is specified in the order, but such an order may not require the Authority to disclose any information falling within section 31(2)(b) of this Act.

(2) The court must not make an order under subsection (1) above unless it is satisfied that the interests of justice require it to do so, taking into account—

(a) any representations made by any individual who may be affected by the disclosure, and

(b) the welfare of the child, if under 18 years old, and of any other person under that age who may be affected by the disclosure.

(3) If the proceedings before the court are civil proceedings, it—

(a) may direct that the whole or any part of the proceedings on the application for an order under subsection (2) above shall be heard in camera, and

(b) if it makes such an order, may then or later direct that the whole or any part of any later stage of the proceedings shall be heard in camera.

(4) An application for a direction under subsection (3) above shall be heard in camera unless the court otherwise directs.

35.—(1) Where for the purpose of instituting proceedings under section 1 of the Congenital Disabilities (Civil Liability) Act 1976 (civil liability to child born disabled) it is necessary to identify a person who would or might be the parent of a child but for sections 27 to 29 of this Act, the court may, on the application of the child, make an order requiring the Authority to disclose any information contained in the register kept in pursuance of section 31 of this Act identifying that person.

Disclosure in interests of justice: congenital disabilities, etc. 1976 c. 28.

(2) Where, for the purposes of any action for damages in Scotland (including any such action which is likely to be brought) in which the damages claimed consist of or include damages or solatium in respect of personal injury (including any disease and any impairment of physical or mental condition), it is necessary to identify a person who would or might be the parent of a child but for sections 27 to 29 of this Act, the court may, on the application of any party to the action or, if the proceedings have not been commenced, the prospective pursuer, make an order requiring the Authority to disclose any information contained in the register kept in pursuance of section 31 of this Act identifying that person.

(3) Subsections (2) to (4) of section 34 of this Act apply for the purposes of this section as they apply for the purposes of that.

(4) After section 4(4) of the Congenital Disabilities (Civil Liability) Act 1976 there is inserted—

'(4A) In any case where a child carried by a woman as the result of the placing in her of an embryo or of sperm and eggs or her artificial insemination is born disabled, any reference in section I of this Act to a parent includes a reference to a person who would be a parent but for sections 27 to 29 of the Human Fertilisation and Embryology Act 1990.'.

Surrogacy

Amendment of Surrogacy Arrangements Act 1985.
1985 c. 49.

36.—(1) After section 1 of the Surrogacy Arrangements Act 1985 there is inserted

'Surrogacy arrangements unenforceable.

1A. No surrogacy arrangement is enforceable by or against any of the persons making it.'

(2) In section 1 of that Act (meaning of 'surrogate mother', etc.)—

(a) in subsection (6), for 'or, as the case may be, embryo insertion' there is substituted 'or of the placing in her of an embryo, of an egg in the process of fertilisation or of sperm and eggs, as the case may be,', and

(b) in subsection (9), the words from 'and whether' to the end are repealed.

. . .

Civil liability to child with disability.
1976 c. 28.

44.—(1) After section 1 of the Congenital Disabilities (Civil Liability) Act 1976 (civil liability to child born disabled) there is inserted—

'Extension Of section 1 to cover infertility treatments.

1A.—(1) In any case where—

(a) a child carried by a woman as the result of the placing in her of an embryo or of sperm and eggs or her artificial insemination is born disabled,

(b) the disability results from an act or omission in the course of the selection, or the keeping or use outside the body, of the embryo carried by her or of the gametes used to bring about the creation of the embryo, and

(c) a person is under this section answerable to the child in respect of the act or omission,

the child's disabilities are to be regarded as damage resulting from the wrongful act of that person and actionable accordingly at the suit of the child.

(2) Subject to subsection (3) below and the applied provisions of section 1 of this Act, a person (here referred to as 'the defendant') is answerable to the child if he was liable in tort to one or both of

the parents (here referred to as 'the parent or parents concerned') or would, if sued in due time, have been so; and it is no answer that there could not have been such liability because the parent or parents concerned suffered no actionable injury, if there was a breach of legal duty which, accompanied by injury, would have given rise to the liability.

(3) The defendant is not under this section answerable to the child if at the time the embryo, or the sperm and eggs, are placed in the woman or the time of her insemination (as the case may be) either or both of the parents knew the risk of their child being born disabled (that is to say, the particular risk created by the act or omission).

(4) Subsections (5) to (7) of section 1 of this Act apply for the purposes of this section as they apply for the purposes of that but as if references to the parent or the parent affected were references to the parent or parents concerned.'

(2) In section 4 of that Act (interpretation, etc)—

(a) at the end of subsection (2) there is inserted—

'and references to embryos shall be construed in accordance with section 1 of the Human Fertilisation and Embryology Act 1990',

(b) in subsection (3), after 'section 1' there is inserted '1A', and

(c) in subsection (4), for 'either' there is substituted 'any'.

1c   Schedule 3: Consents to Use of Gametes or Embryos

Consent

1. A consent under this Schedule must be given in writing and, in this Schedule, 'effective consent' means a consent under this Schedule which has not been withdrawn.

2.—(1) A consent to the use of any embryo must specify one or more of the following purposes—

(a) use in providing treatment services to the person giving consent, or that person and another specified person together,

(b) use in providing treatment services to persons not including the person giving consent, or

(c) use for the purposes of any project of research,

and may specify conditions subject to which the embryo may be so used.

(2) A consent to the storage of any gametes or any embryo must—

(a) specify the maximum period of storage (if less than the statutory storage period), and

(b) state what is to be done with the gametes or embryo if the person who gave the consent dies or is unable because of incapacity to vary the terms of the consent or to revoke it,

and may specify conditions subject to which the gametes or embryo may remain in storage.

(3) A consent under this Schedule must provide for such other matters as the Authority may specify in directions.

(4) A consent under this Schedule may apply—

(a) to the use or storage of a particular embryo, or

(b) in the case of a person providing gametes, to the use or storage of any embryo whose creation may be brought about using those gametes,

and in the paragraph (b) case the terms of the consent may be varied, or the consent may be withdrawn, in accordance with this Schedule either generally or in relation to a particular embryo or particular embryos.

Procedure for giving consent

3.—(1) Before a person gives consent under this Schedule—

(a) he must be given a suitable opportunity to receive proper counselling about the implications of taking the proposed steps, and

(b) he must be provided with such relevant information as is proper.

(2) Before a person gives consent under this Schedule he must be informed of the effect of paragraph 4 below.

Variation and withdrawal of consent

4.—(1) The terms of any consent under this Schedule may from time to time be varied, and the consent may be withdrawn, by notice given by the person who gave the consent to the person keeping the gametes or embryo to which the consent is relevant.

(2) The terms of any consent to the use of any embryo cannot be varied, and such consent cannot be withdrawn, once the embryo has been used—

(a) in providing treatment services, or

(b) for the purposes of any project of research.

Use of gametes for treatment of others

5.—(1) A person's gametes must not be used for the purposes of treatment services unless there is an effective consent by that person to their being so used and they are used in accordance with the terms of the consent.

(2) A person's gametes must not be received for use for those purposes unless there is an effective consent by that person to their being so used.

(3) This paragraph does not apply to the use of a person's gametes for the purpose of that person, or that person and another together, receiving treatment services.

In vitro fertilisation and subsequent use of embryo

6.—(1) A person's gametes must not be used to bring about the creation of any embryo *in vitro* unless there is an effective consent by that person to any embryo the creation of which may be brought about with the use of those gametes being used for one or more of the purposes mentioned in paragraph 2(1) above.

(2) An embryo the creation of which was brought about *in vitro* must not be received by any person unless there is an effective consent by each person whose gametes were used to bring about the creation of the embryo to the use for one or more of the purposes mentioned in paragraph 2(1) above of the embryo.

(3) An embryo the creation of which was brought about *in vitro* must not be used for any purpose unless there is an effective consent by each person whose gametes were used to bring about the creation of the embryo to the use for that purpose of the embryo and the embryo is used in accordance with those consents.

(4) Any consent required by this paragraph is in addition to any consent that may be required by paragraph 5 above.

Embryos obtained by lavage, etc.

7.—(1) An embryo taken from a woman must not be used for any purpose unless there is an effective consent by her to the use of the embryo for that purpose and it is used in accordance with the consent.

(2) An embryo taken from a woman must not be received by any person for use for any purpose unless there is an effective consent by her to the use of the embryo for that purpose.

(3) This paragraph does not apply to the use, for the purpose of

providing a woman with treatment services, of an embryo taken from her.

Storage of gametes and embryos

8.—(1) A person's gametes must not be kept in storage unless there is an effective consent by that person to their storage and they are stored in accordance with the consent.

(2) An embryo the creation of which was brought about *in vitro* must not be kept in storage unless there is an effective consent, by each person whose gametes were used to bring about the creation of the embryo, to the storage of the embryo and the embryo is stored in accordance with those consents.

(3) An embryo taken from a woman must not be kept in storage unless there is an effective consent by her to its storage and it is stored in accordance with the consent.

Appendix 2
Abortion Act 1967: Chapter 87

An Act to amend and clarify the law relating to termination of pregnancy by registered medical practitioners. [27th October 1967]

. . .

1.—(1) Subject to the provisions of this section, a person shall not be guilty of an offence under the law relating to abortion when a pregnancy is terminated by a registered medical practitioner if two registered medical practitioners are of the opinion, formed in good faith— {Medical termination of pregnancy.}

   (a) that the continuance of the pregnancy would involve risk to the life of the pregnant woman, or of injury to the physical or mental health of the pregnant woman or any existing children of her family, greater than if the pregnancy were terminated; or

   (b) that there is a substantial risk that if the child were born it would suffer from such physical or mental abnormalities as to be seriously handicapped.

(2) In determining whether the continuance of a pregnancy would involve such risk of injury to health as is mentioned in paragraph (a) of subsection (1) of this section, account may be taken of the pregnant woman's actual or reasonably foreseeable environment.

(3) Except as provided by subsection (4) of this section, any treatment for the termination of pregnancy must be carried out in a hospital vested in the Minister of Health or the Secretary of State under the National Health Service Acts, or in a place for the time being approved for the purposes of this section by the said Minister or the Secretary of State.

(4) Subsection (3) of this section, and so much of subsection (1) as relates to the opinion of two registered medical practitioners, shall not apply to the termination of a pregnancy by a registered medical practitioner in a case where he is of the opinion, formed in good faith, that the termination is immediately necessary to save the life or to prevent grave permanent injury to the physical or mental health of the pregnant woman.

Notification.

2.—(1) The Minister of Health in respect of England and Wales, and the Secretary of State in respect of Scotland, shall by statutory instrument make regulations to provide—

(a) for requiring any such opinion as is referred to in section 1 of this Act to be certified by the practitioners or practitioner concerned in such form and at such time as may be prescribed by the regulations, and for requiring the preservation and disposal of certificates made for the purposes of the regulations;

(b) for requiring any registered medical practitioner who terminates a pregnancy to give notice of the termination and such other information relating to the termination as may be so prescribed;

(c) for prohibiting the disclosure, except to such persons or for such purposes as may be so prescribed, of notices given or information furnished pursuant to the regulations.

(2) The information furnished in pursuance of regulations made by virtue of paragraph (b) of subsection (1) of this section shall be notified solely to the Chief Medical Officers of the Ministry of Health and the Scottish Home and Health Department respectively.

(3) Any person who wilfully contravenes or wilfully fails to comply with the requirements of regulations under subsection (1) of this section shall be liable on summary conviction to a fine not exceeding one hundred pounds.

. . .

Application of Act to visiting forces etc.

3.—(1) In relation to the termination of a pregnancy in a case where the following conditions are satisfied, that is to say—

(a) the treatment for termination of the pregnancy was carried out in a hospital controlled by the proper authorities of a body to which this section applies; and

(b) the pregnant woman had at the time of the treatment a relevant association with that body; and

(c) the treatment was carried out by a registered medical practitioner or a person who at the time of the treatment was a member of that body appointed as a medical practitioner for that body by the proper authorities of that body,

this Act shall have effect as if any reference in section 1 to a registered medical practitioner and to a hospital vested in a Minister under the National Health Service Acts included respectively a reference to such a person as is mentioned in paragraph (c) of this subsection and to a hospital controlled as aforesaid, and as if section 2 were omitted.

. . .

4.—(1) Subject to subsection (2) of this section, no person shall be under any duty, whether by contract or by any statutory or other legal requirement, to participate in any treatment authorised by this Act to which he has a conscientious objection: Conscientious objection to participation in treatment.

Provided that in any legal proceedings the burden of proof of conscientious objection shall rest on the person claiming to rely on it.

(2) Nothing in subsection (1) of this section shall affect any duty to participate in treatment which is necessary to save the life or to prevent grave permanent injury to the physical or mental health of a pregnant woman.

(3) In any proceedings before a court in Scotland, a statement on oath by any person to the effect that he has a conscientious objection to participating in any treatment authorised by this Act shall be sufficient evidence for the purpose of discharging the burden of proof imposed upon him by subsection (1) of this section.

. . .

7.—(1) This Act may be cited as the Abortion Act 1967. Short title, commencement and extent.

(2) This Act shall come into force on the expiration of the period of six months beginning with the date on which it is passed.

(3) This Act does not extend to Northern Ireland.

Appendix 3
The Abortion Regulations 1991

Citation and commencement

1.—(1) These Regulations may be cited as the Abortion Regulations 1991, and shall come into force on 1st April 1991.

(2) These Regulations extend to England and Wales only.

Interpretation

2. In these Regulations 'the Act' means the Abortion Act 1967 and 'practitioner' means a registered medical practitioner.

Certificate of opinion

3.—(1) Any opinion to which section 1 of the Act refers shall be certified—

   (a) in the case of a pregnancy terminated in accordance with section 1(1) of the Act, in the form set out in Part I of Schedule 1 to these Regulations, and

   (b) in the case of a pregnancy terminated in accordance with section 1(4) of the Act, in the form set out in Part II of that Schedule.

(2) Any certificate of an opinion referred to in section 1(1) of the Act shall be given before the commencement of the treatment for the termination of the pregnancy to which it relates.

(3) Any certificate of an opinion referred to in section 1(4) of the Act shall be given before the commencement of the treatment for the termination of the pregnancy to which it relates or, if that is not reasonably practicable, not later than 24 hours after such termination.

(4) Any such certificate as is referred to in paragraphs (2) and (3) of this regulation shall be preserved by the practitioner who terminated the pregnancy to which it relates for a period of not less than three years beginning with the date of the termination.

(5) A certificate which is no longer to be preserved shall be destroyed by the person in whose custody it then is.

Notice of termination of pregnancy and information relating to the termination

4.—(1) Any practitioner who terminates a pregnancy in England or Wales shall give to the appropriate Chief Medical Officer—

(a) notice of the termination, and

(b) such other information relating to the termination as is specified in the form set out in Schedule 2 to these Regulations,

and shall do so by sending them to him in a sealed envelope within 7 days of the termination.

(2) The appropriate Chief Medical Officer is—

(a) where the pregnancy was terminated in England, the Chief Medical Officer of the Department of Health, Richmond House, Whitehall, London, SW1A 2NS; or

(b) where the pregnancy was terminated in Wales, the Chief Medical Officer of the Welsh Office, Cathays Park, Cardiff, CF1 3NQ.

Restriction on disclosure of information

5. A notice given or any information furnished to a Chief Medical Officer in pursuance of these Regulations shall not be disclosed except that disclosure may be made—

(a) for the purposes of carrying out their duties—

(i) to an officer of the Department of Health authorised by the Chief Medical Officer of that Department, or to an officer of the Welsh Office authorised by the Chief Medical Officer of that Office, as the case may be, or

(ii) to the Registrar General or a member of his staff authorised by him: or

(b) for the purposes of carrying out his duties in relation to offences under the Act or the law relating to abortion, to the Director of Public Prosecutions or a member of his staff authorised by him; or

(c) for the purposes of investigating whether an offence has been committed under the Act or the law relating to abortion, to a police officer not below the rank of superintendent or a person authorised by him; or

(d) pursuant to a court order, for the purposes of proceedings which have begun; or

(e) for the purposes of bona fide scientific research; or

(f) to the practitioner who terminated the pregnancy; or

(g) to a practitioner, with the consent in writing of the woman whose pregnancy was terminated; or

(h) when requested by the President of the General Medical Council for the purpose of investigating whether there has been serious professional misconduct by a practitioner, to the President of the General Medical Council or a member of its staff authorised by him.

. . .

EXPLANATORY NOTE

(This note is not part of the Regulations)

These Regulations (which extend to England and Wales) are made under section 2 of the Abortion Act 1967, and replace the Abortion Regulations 1968 and the three sets of amending regulations. These Regulations make new provision to take account in particular of the amendments to the Abortion Act 1967 made by section 37 of the Human Fertilisation and Embryology Act 1990 (c.37), including the new grounds for abortion introduced by those amendments.

Appendix 4
Sperm and Egg Donors and the Law

Sperm and egg donors and the law

Assisted conception techniques allow some couples who could not otherwise have their own child to do so by using eggs or sperm donated by other people. This leaflet sets out to answer some questions which arise about the legal position of sperm and egg donors since the Human Fertilisation and Embryology Act 1990 (HFE Act) came into effect on 1 August 1991. The HFE Act provides a legal framework to protect the interests of the donors, any children born and the legal parents of those children.

More information about becoming a donor and an explanation of the procedures involved is given in two leaflets: 'Important Information for Semen Donors' published by the Royal College of Obstetricians and Gynaecologists: and 'Egg Donation' published by the Human Fertilisation and Embryology Authority (HFEA). Both of these are available from the HFEA. In addition all centres recruiting donors will be able to give you information and will offer you counselling.

Who will be the legal parents of a child born from your donation?

It is the law that the woman receiving treatment and her husband or male partner being treated with her will be the legal parents, although you will be the genetic parent of any child born. You will have no legal relationship to any child born, nor will you have any legal rights over or obligations to any child born. In the same way any child born will have no legal relationship with you, no rights over you and no obligations to you.

Information about you

Once you decide to become an egg or sperm donor the clinic must ask you for personal details. This is both for its own records and to send to the HFEA. By law, donors' names and dates of birth have to be given to the Authority which holds them on its confidential information register. In addition non-identifying information such as eye colour, hair colour, occupation and interests is also held on the register.

Why the HFEA has to know your name and date of birth

The HFEA has to know this information about you to safeguard the interests of children born as a result of your donation. The HFEA has a legal duty under the HFE Act to tell adults who ask whether they were born as a result of treatment using donated eggs or sperm. People aged 16 or over, who ask, can be told whether they could be related to someone they want to marry. Without basic identifying information (name and age) the Authority could not establish whether or not there is a genetic (or blood) relationship between people who wish to marry. Fulfilling this legal duty will not involve the disclosure of any information about you.

Your name will be kept confidential

The HFEA has a standard form it supplies to clinics which will be used to record the information about you. One copy of the form will be kept securely at the clinic and one copy will be sent to the Authority and the information from it stored securely on our computerised register.

The HFE Act 1990 makes unauthorised disclosure of donors' names a criminal offence with a maximum penalty of 2 years' imprisonment and a fine. The law does not allow children who may apply for information from the HFEA register to know the identity of current or past donors. The only people allowed to know a donor's name are members and employees of the Authority and staff covered by an HFEA licence at the clinic or storage centre.

The only exception to this is as follows: a child may be able to sue a donor and a clinic for damages, if the child was born with a disability as a result of the donor's failure to disclose inherited disease. Legal action is extremely unlikely, provided a donor is open and honest about his or her medical and family history. Should this situation arise, in England, Wales or Northern Ireland, a court of law may require the HFEA to disclose the name of a donor so that a child may bring proceedings under the Congenital Disabilities (Civil Liability) Act 1976. In Scotland, a court order may require the HFEA to release the name of a donor so that a child may sue for damages for personal injury. In such a situation the clinic or people covered by an HFEA licence may have to defend legal proceedings or may bring related proceedings for compensation against the donor. In these two circumstances a clinic may disclose the identity of a donor.

Why the HFEA collects additional information

At present no information whatsoever about you may be given to children born following treatment with your donated sperm or eggs. In the future Parliament may decide that some details may be given to those children if they apply to the Authority. But even if this happens the child will not be told your name because the HFE Act 1990 specifically prevents the disclosure of the names of current and past donors to offspring.

The HFEA collects additional, non-identifying information because it may be helpful to children born following treatment with your eggs or sperm who want to gain some insight to their genetic origins. With this in mind, the Authority collects general information about what you look like. It also offers you the opportunity to describe yourself and your talents and interests more fully in your own words if you think that could be helpful to a child born as a result of your donation. If Parliament in the future makes this decision, such a child after reaching the age of 18, could contact the HFEA for the information.

So except where donation is intentionally between people known to each other, current and past donors will remain anonymous to the couples treated with their eggs or sperm, and to the children who may be born as a result of that treatment. And, as explained above, no information whatsoever about any particular donor may be released to the general public.

Other legal aspects of sperm and egg donation

How will your sperm or eggs be used?

The law requires that you give written consent to the use and storage of your sperm or eggs, and of any embryos produced with them. This consent may be for treating others and/or for a research project. The HFE Act says that you must give informed consent. In other words, you must be given information about the process and implications of donation, including the duration of storage, and you must have been offered counselling. When you give consent, the Act allows you to attach conditions to the donation, for example, you may wish to specify to whom you wish to give your eggs or sperm. However, if a donor sets conditions which are too stringent, the clinic may decide not to accept him or her as a donor.

In addition, clinics must ask about previous donations you may have made, and if necessary must obtain your consent to contact other clinics involved or your GP about any relevant medical history.

Can you get counselling about becoming a donor?

Yes. The clinic is obliged by law to offer you counselling before you consent to the use and storage of your sperm or eggs, and any embryos produced with them. You do not have to accept the offer of counselling but it provides an opportunity to discuss with an impartial person any concerns you may have. These could be concerns about any aspects of donation, including the implications of becoming a donor for you and your family.

This text is reproduced from a leaflet published in 1992 by the Human Fertilisation and Embryology Authority, from whom further information on all aspects of assisted conception is available. The address of the Authority appears in Appendix 5.

Appendix 5

Resources and Organisations

British Fertility Society (affiliated with the International Federation of Fertility Societies)
BFS Secretary's Office, 2nd Floor, Room 2/62, Birmingham Maternity Hospital, Edgbaston, Birmingham, B15 2TG
Tel. 0121–627 2696; Fax. 0121–414 1576

British Infertility Counselling Association
10 Alwyne Place, London, N1 2NL
Tel. 0171–354 8927

British Pregnancy Advisory Service
Austy Manor, Wootten Wawen, Solihull, West Midlands, B95 6DA
Tel. 015642–3225

Child (support and information for those with infertility problems)
PO Box 154, Hounslow, Middlesex, TW3 0EZ
Tel. 0181–571 4376

COTS (Childlessness Overcome Through Surrogacy)
Loandhu Cottage, Gruids, Lairg, Sutherland, IV27 4EF, Scotland
Tel. and Fax. 01549–2401

Family Planning Association
27 Mortimer Street, London, W1N 7RJ
Tel. 0171–636 7866

Human Fertilisation and Embryology Authority
Paxton House, 30 Artillery Lane, London, E1 7LS
Tel. 0171–377 5077; Fax. 0171–377 1871

ISSUE (The National Fertility Association) Limited
509 Aldridge Road, Great Barr, Birmingham, B44 8NA
Tel. 0121–344 4414; Fax. 0121–344 4336

Multiple Births Foundation
Institute of Obstetrics and Gynaecology, Queen Charlotte's and Chelsea Hospital, Goldhawk Road, London, W6 0XG
Tel. 0181–740 3519

Needs (National Egg and Embryo Donation Society)
Regional IVF Unit, St Mary's Hospital, Whitworth Park, Manchester, M13 0JH
Tel. 0161–276 6000

Planned Parenthood Federation of America
810 Seventh Avenue, New York, NY, USA
Tel. 212–841 7800

Pregnancy Advisory Service
11–13 Charlotte Street, London, W1P 1HD
Tel. 0171–637 8962

Resolve (counselling, referral and support for infertile couples)
1310 Broadway, Somerville, Massachusetts 02144, USA
Tel. 617–623 0744

Women's Health and Reproductive Rights Information Centre
52–54 Featherstone Street, London, EC1Y
Tel. 0171–251 6332

References

Abbey, Antonia, Andrews, Frank M. and Halman, Jill L. (1991) 'The importance of social relationships for infertile couples' well-being', in Annette L. Stanton and Christine Dunkel-Schetter (eds), *Infertility. Perspectives from Stress and Coping Research*. New York: Plenum.

Abbey, Antonia, Halman, Jill L. and Andrews, Frank M. (1992) 'Psychosocial treatment, and demographic predictors of the stress associated with infertility', *Fertility and Sterility*, 57(1): 122–8.

Adler, Nancy (1991) 'Foreword' in Annette L. Stanton and Christine Dunkel-Schetter (eds), *Infertility. Perspectives from Stress and Coping Research*. New York: Plenum.

Allen, Isobel (1985) *Counselling Services for Sterilisation, Vasectomy and Termination of Pregnancy*. London: Policy Studies Institute.

Berg, Barbara J. and Wilson, John F. (1990) 'Psychiatric morbidity in the infertile population: a reconceptualisation', *Fertility and Sterility*, 53(4): 654.

Blumberg, Bruce (1984) 'The emotional implications of prenatal diagnosis', in Alan E.H. Emery and Ian Pullen (eds), *Psychological Aspects of Genetic Counselling*. London: Academic Press.

Bonnicksen, Andrea L. (1989) *In Vitro Fertilization. Building Policy from Laboratories to Legislatures*. New York and Oxford: Columbia University Press.

Bowlby, J. (1980) *Attachment and Loss: Loss, Sadness, and Depression*, vol. III. New York: Basic Books.

Brebner, Cecilia M., Sharp, John D. and Stone, Frederick H. (1985) *The Role of Infertility in Adoption*. Discussion Series no. 7. London: British Agencies for Adoption and Fostering.

Chadwick, Ruth F. (ed.) (1992) *Ethics, Reproduction and Genetic Control*. London: Routledge.

Crowe, Micheal and Ridley, Jane (1990) *Therapy with Couples. A Behavioural-Systems Approach to Marital and Sexual Problems*. Oxford: Blackwell Scientific.

Cusine, Douglas J. (1988/1990) *New Reproductive Techniques. A Legal Perspective*. Dartmouth.

Doyle, Kathy and Delany, Linda (1991) 'Infertility management in HIV positive couples: a dilemma', *British Medical Journal*, 302: 1447–50.

Dunkel-Schetter, Christine and Lobel, Marci (1991) 'Psychological reactions to infertility', in Annette L. Stanton and Christine Dunkel-Schetter (eds), *Infertility. Perspectives from Stress and Coping Research*. New York: Plenum.

Family Planning Association (1994a) *Abortion: Statistical Trends*, Factsheet 6A, Table 6.7. London: FPA.

Family Planning Association (1994b) *Abortion: Legal and Ethical Issues*. Factsheet 6B. London: FPA.

Golombok, S., Cook, R., Bish, R. and Murray, C. (1993) 'Quality of parenting in families created by the new reproductive technologies: a brief report of preliminary findings', *Journal of Psychosomatic Obstetrics and Gynaecology*, 14 (Special Issue): 17–22.

Gottman, John (1991) 'Predicting the longitudinal course of marriages', *Journal of Marital and Family Therapy*, 17(1): 3–7.

HFEA (1990) *Code of Practice*. London: Human Fertilisation and Embryology Authority.

HFEA (1994) Second Annual Report. London: Human Fertilisation and Embryology Authority.

Hull, Micheal (in collaboration with Study Group) (1993) *The Infertility Information Pack*. Sponsored by Serono Laboratories Ltd.

Inskipp, Francesca (1986) *Counselling: the Trainer's Handbook*. The Effective Trainer Series. Cambridge: National Extension College.

Jones, Steve (1994) *The Language of Genes*. London: Flamingo.

King's Fund (1991) *Counselling for Regulated Infertility Treatments*. A Report of the King's Fund Centre Counselling Committee. London: The King's Fund.

Kirkland, A., Power, M., Burton, G., Baber, R., Studd, J. and Abdalla, H. (1992) 'Comparison of attitudes of donors and recipients to oocyte donation', *Human Reproduction*, 7(3): 355–7.

Kubler-Ross, Elisabeth (1973) *On Death and Dying*. London: Tavistock.

Leick, Nini and Davidsen-Nielsen, Marianne (1991) *Healing Pain. Attachment, Loss and Grief Therapy*. London: Routledge.

le Pere, Dorothy (1988) 'Vulnerability to crises during the life cycle of the adoptive family', in Deborah Valentine (ed.), *Infertility and Adoption. A Guide for Social Work Practice*. New York and London: The Haworth Press.

Mariner, Wendy K. (1992) 'The Supreme Court, abortion, and the jurisprudence of class', (Health Law and Ethics), *American Journal of Public Health*, 82(11): 1556–61.

Mason, Mary-Claire (1993) *Male Infertility – Men Talking*. London and New York: Routledge.

MMWR (Morbidity and Mortality Weekly Report) (1993) CDC Surveillance Summaries. Special Focus: Surveillance for Reproductive Health. US Department of Health and Human Services: Public Health Service. Centers for Disease Control and Prevention, vol. 42, N.SS-6. Atlanta: Abortion Surveillance. United States, 1990.

Morgan, Derek and Lee, Robert G. (1991) *Blackstone's Guide to the Human Fertilisation and Embryology Act 1990. Abortion and Embryo Research, The New Law*. London: Blackstone Press.

Mosher, William and Pratt, William (1991) 'Fecundity and infertility in the United States: incidence and trends', *Fertility and Sterility*, 56(2): 193.

Mostyn, B. (1992) *Infertility. Guidelines for Practice*. London: Royal College of Obstetrics and Gynaecology Press.

OPCS (1992) Monitor AB94/1. London: Office of Population Censuses and Surveys/ Government Statistical Service.

Paintin, David (1992) 'Abortion in first trimester', *British Medical Journal*, 305: 967–8.

Power, M., Baber, R., Abdullah, H., Kirkland, A., Leonard, T. and Studd, J.W.W. (1990) 'A comparison of the attitudes of volunteer donors and infertile patient donors on an ovum donation programme', *Human Reproduction*, 5(3): 352–5.

Rantala, Maija-Liisa and Koskimies, Aarne Iivari (1988) 'Sexual behaviour of infertile couples', *International Journal of Fertility*, 33(1): 26–30.

RCOG (1992) *Infertility. Guidelines for Practice*. London: Royal College of Obstetricians and Gynaecologists Press.

Reading, Anthony E. (1991) 'Psychological intervention and infertility', in Annette L. Stanton and Christine Dunkel-Schetter (eds), *Infertility. Perspectives from Stress and Coping Research*. New York: Plenum.

Savage, W. and Francome, C. (1989) 'Gynaecologists' attitudes to abortion', *Lancet*, 2: 1323–4.

Shapiro, Constance Hoenk (1988) *Infertility and Pregnancy Loss. A Guide for Helping Professionals*. San Francisco: Jossey-Bass.

Stanton, Annette L. (1991) 'Cognitive appraisals, coping processes, and adjustment to infertility', in Annette L. Stanton and Christine Dunkel-Schetter (eds), *Infertility. Perspectives from Stress and Coping Research*. New York: Plenum.

Stanton, Annette L. and Dunkel-Schetter, Christine (eds) (1991) 'Psychological adjustment to infertility. An overview of conceptual approaches', in *Infertility. Perspectives from Stress and Coping Research*. New York: Plenum.

Steiner, Claude (1986) *When a Man loves a Woman. Sexual and Emotional Literacy for the Modern Man*. New York: Grove Press.

Tennen, Howard, Affleck, Glenn and Mendola, Richard (1991) 'Causal explanations for infertility: their relation to control appraisals and psychological adjustment', in Annette L. Stanton and Christine Dunkel-Schetter (eds), *Infertility. Perspectives from Stress and Coping Research*. New York: Plenum.

Walby, C. and Symons, B. (1990) *Who am I?* London: British Agencies for Adoption and Fostering.

Warnock Report (1984) *Report of the Committee of Inquiry into Fertilisation and Embryology*. Cmnd no. 9314. London: HMSO.

Worden, William J. (1991) *Grief Counselling and Grief Therapy. A Handbook for the Mental Health Practitioner*, 2nd edn. London: Routledge.

Index